Voices of the Silenced

Voices
of the
Silenced

*The Responsible Self
in a Marginalized Community*

Darryl M. Trimiew

*The Pilgrim Press
Cleveland, Ohio*

The Pilgrim Press, Cleveland, Ohio 44115
© 1993 by Darryl M. Trimiew

The following publishers have generously given permission to use extended quotations from copyrighted works: From Ida B. Wells-Barnett, *Crusade for Justice,* ed. Alfreda Duster, © 1970 by The University of Chicago Press, reprinted by permission of The University of Chicago Press; from Francis J. Grimké, *The Works of Francis J. Grimké: Addresses Mainly Personal and Racial,* ed. Carter G. Woodson, reprinted by permission of The Associated Publishers, Inc.; from H. Richard Niebuhr, *The Responsible Self,* © 1963 by Florence Niebuhr, reprinted by permission of HarperCollins Publishers; from Edwin S. Redkey, ed., *Respect Black: The Writings and Speeches of Henry McNeal Turner,* reprinted by permission of Ayer Co. Publishers; from H. Richard Niebuhr, *The Meaning of Revelation,* © 1967 by Macmillan Publishing Company, reprinted by permission of Macmillan Publishing Company; from Julio De Santa Ana, *Towards a Church of the Poor: The Work of an Ecumenical Group on the Church and the Poor,* reprinted by permission of Orbis Books.

Biblical quotations are from the New Revised Standard Version of the Bible, © 1989 by the Division of Christian Education of the National Council of the Churches of Christ in the U.S.A., and are used by permission

Library of Congress Cataloging-in-Publication Data

Trimiew, Darryl M., 1952–
    Voices of the silenced : the responsible self in a
marginalized community / Darryl M. Trimiew.
      p.   cm.
    Includes bibliographical references and index.
      ISBN 0-8298-0962-7. — ISBN 0-8298-0967-8 (pbk.)
      1. Niebuhr, H. Richard (Helmut Richard), 1894–1962. The responsible
self. 2. Christian ethics. 3. Responsibility. 4. Marginality, Social—Moral and
ethical aspects. 5. Turner, Henry McNeal, 1834-1915. 6. Wells-Barnett, Ida B.,
1862–1931. 7. Grimké, Francis J. (Francis James), 1850-1937. 8. Afro-Americans—
Religion. 9. Liberation theology. I. Title.
BJ1251.N523T75   1993
241'.04—dc20   93-19178
                CIP

Contents

5-3-9人

Acknowledgments

The ensuing book issues from a process of reflection that began in my youth. As a resident of Newark, New Jersey, during the catastrophic riots of 1967–68, I was amazed and appalled by the sudden collapse of a troubled yet viable community. My subsequent educational odyssey through college and law school was first, an attempt to understand my community, and second, an effort to acquire useful skills with which I could contribute to the revitalization of it.

The practice of law revealed to me many of the problems caused by widespread acts of irresponsibility. The basically ineffectual responses of the church to the underlying problems of urban unrest compelled me to question the adequacy of current ministerial preparation and forced me, finally, to relinquish my law practice and to retool in seminary and graduate school in preparation for an educational ministry in theological education. In graduate school, I studied with E. Clinton Gardner and was mentored by the late Romney Moseley, who is sorely missed. Both scholars were concerned with the problem of moral responsibility. Dr. Gardner quickened my interest in the responsibilist approach and should be credited with instilling in me a deep appreciation of the work of H. Richard Niebuhr. Any misreadings of the Niebuhrian texts are my own fault: Dr. Gardner did his best. The present study is an attempt to criticize, correct, and to extend Niebuhr's basic approach by a marginalized writer working from a different social location than that of Niebuhr and writing with knowledge of historical circumstances that Niebuhr never lived to see.

I have also been deeply influenced by my studies with Noel Erskine, Jürgen Moltmann, and José Míguez Bonino, all of whom I therefore thank. A special word of thanks must go to Robert Michael Franklin whose recent book, *Liberating Visions*, gave me the structural format for the present work. Two other scholars, Theodore Walker and Emily Townes, deserve special mention for reading some of the drafts of this work and offering very helpful criticisms of it. I also am indebted to the students of my Religion and Morality class, given in spring 1991. My idea for the book crystallized while teaching this class. In addition, I am grateful to Brite Divinity School and its generous summer stipend program, which enabled me to devote the summer of 1992 to this work, as well as to my dedicated research assistant, Beverly Lawson. I am also pleased to record a special word of thanks to my loving wife, Dolores Marie Trimiew, for her companionship and support throughout our marriage and particularly during the writing of this work. Indeed, she has been my special responsible self with whom I am raising two conscientious and loving children, Rehema and Rubani, my inspirations.

This book is dedicated to William ("Bill") Thomas, an African-American insurance salesman whose greatest gifts lay not in insurance sales but in his ability to act responsibly in his marginalized community. Bill came up the hard way. After considerable sacrifice, at a time when black men were nearly barred from college education, he obtained professional competency in the field of chemistry. He married and settled down, but disaster soon struck in the form of a traffic accident, as a result of which both of his legs had to be amputated. Bill adjusted well and began to sell insurance, but, more important, he continued helping others as an effective layperson at Waverly Avenue Presbyterian Church, a small African-American congregation.

Bill never left his community or his calling. His gift lay in his ability to perceive the true nature of his community's problems and to get people talking and working together towards a solution. An unforgettable presence, Bill had a cheeriness and patience that never failed to raise your spirits. In his presence you felt that you mattered and that God cared about you because Bill did. Being a member of a racial minority, severely physically challenged, never in robust health, but always level-headed, open-hearted and morally sound, he convinced those around him who were in marginalized circumstances that God was moving in our midst and that we, empowered by God, could transform ourselves and the world. Indeed, from Bill you came to believe that marginalized people have power, because all power is delegated to all people from a God that loves us. The power of Bill's actions and example convinced this writer that marginalized people could be effective agents of God in the transformation of the world. Thus this book moves from Bill's personal example to an exploration of how historical figures in marginalized communities have acted responsibly with regard to moral conflicts. This reflection on moral responsibility and justifiable praxis is designed to aid Christians in their struggle to live morally responsible lives.

Introduction

"Responsibility affirms: God is acting in all actions upon you. So respond to all actions upon you as to respond to his action."[1] This admonition, central to H. Richard Niebuhr's approach to Christian social ethics, is deeply inspiring and, at the same time, deeply troubling. It inspires because it summons the believer to respond to God in faith under any and all circumstances. Nevertheless, it troubles one's soul because it encourages believers to interpret all actions, no matter how oppressive, as the providence of God. This hermeneutical problem is the primary quandary in the modern Christian world. Niebuhr's complex call for response requires a penetrating analysis of a world in which, on a daily basis, forty thousand people starve to death. Any "responsible self" must wonder how God is acting in the world, and what God may have planned for him or her. This book attempts to answer that question.[2]

In America, studies in Christian ethics invariably acquaint one with the work of H. Richard Niebuhr. In 1963, Niebuhr's lifelong study of how morally capable people are obliged to act responsibly toward others was published posthumously as *The Responsible Self*. This work has proven enormously influential. Niebuhr eschewed both deontology and teleology; he offered a third, more flexible way of dealing with moral dilemmas: the responsibilist approach—the "fitting" response. Yet the very flexibility of Niebuhr's approach, with its contextualism, its lack of prescriptions, casuistry, or easily discernible goals seems, to some of his critics, to give too little attention to the problem of constructing a viable approach to moral living from a Christian perspective.[3]

Other critics have expressed some doubts about the applicability of Niebuhr's approach to many of the life situations that confront people, and it is this criticism that will be addressed herein. In a world of oppression, how does one act responsibly? What forms of action are responsible? In particular, how should marginalized people respond to acts of oppression? A central question arises immediately: Is Niebuhr's "responsible self" an appropriate root metaphor for the masses of marginalized people? From this writer's point of view, Niebuhr's approach, although it contains substantial truth, nevertheless appears to be inadequate.

A review of Niebuhr's work reveals that his symbol functions primarily as an empowered self located in a world that recognizes fully only that self. If this last location is its final one, it does not appear to be a fitting symbol for marginalized people and cannot help us in our struggle for life. Furthermore, if it is not a fitting symbol for the marginalized people of the world, then it is also probably unsuitable for empowered selves who might read Niebuhr's work and wish to be and work in solidarity with the oppressed. Yet even from a marginalized perspective, there is something attractive about Niebuhr's approach that tempts one to work through it to see whether or not its flaws can be removed and its structure employed for ethical reflection with a clear predisposition for liberating oneself and others from the coils of oppression. Can Niebuhr's work be employed as a useful tool, or must it, if it is considered at all, be considered an impediment to the task of liberation?

In this book the attempt is made to correct Niebuhr's flawed work and take it further. It is assumed that Niebuhr's approach can be useful if it is reworked from a marginalized perspective, utilizing a different internal history, a somewhat different value system, and an extension of some of the logic inherent in his work. This is not a new approach to Christian social ethics, but rather an extension of the responsibilist approach that incorporates the theological tradition of liberation theology. The primary difference lies in an explicit recognition that Niebuhr's work is a product of an empowered self that engaged in moral reasoning from a situation and experience of basic sustainability. In contrast, this work is the product of a marginalized self whose social location and sustainability are more tenuous.

It is further posited herein that the struggle to overcome oppression is a more useful epistemological position from which to begin the process of moral reflection than the empowered location. The praxis and moral re-flection of three marginalized moral exemplars will be examined and analyzed to see how they performed in morally appropriate fashions in their marginalized communities. The examination will reveal that the common thread running through the variety of responses consists of the attempt, from a black Christian perspective, to meet the basic needs of the exemplars and their community in ways that did not inherently impugn their human dignity. It is this commitment to helping people meet their basic human needs in ways that leave their dignity unimpaired that is the suggested corrective to Niebuhr's approach and the appropriate extension of his project. The reality of oppression creates a problematic situation for moral reflection at the same time that it forces the moral agent to ask tough questions that Niebuhr never adequately addressed.

THE MARGINALIZED SELF: WHO IS SHE/HE?

First of all, what is meant by the awkward term *marginalization?* A simple definition would be that marginalization is the process by which certain people are pushed from the center of the decision-making process that a society employs to distribute its benefits and burdens, goods and services, merits and demerits. This same process assigns meaning to some issues and people while determining that others are not worthy of consideration. It is a process in which some persons get to speak, but others are constrained to remain silent; in this process, one's social status and life chances are rigidly determined and one's fate and the fate of one's progeny are cast in doubt. Marginalization is an oppressive practice; its perpetrators are perceived as oppressors, and marginalized people feel the need to resist oppression and to escape our intended destinies as mere victims. Marginalization attempts to limit our freedom to act, and it often prevents us from meeting our basic human needs.

In such a setting, is it possible for us to act responsibly? Since this writer considers himself to have suffered oppression and to have engaged in responsible moral action, obviously marginalization cannot, logically speaking, make ethical reflection and moral praxis impossible. Still, nearly all ethicists have insisted that a condition of freedom is necessary for the exercise of moral responsibility. However, by any definition, oppressors have imposed some repressive limitations upon oppressed people's free exercise of agency. Accordingly, how oppressed people can act morally is often problematic. On the other hand, the ability of oppressors to exercise moral responsibility in any fashion appears to be even more problematic since every principle that they hold or employ (as deontologists), and every result or end that they seek to realize (as consequentialists and teleologists), and every response that they make and offer as "appropriate" (as responsibilists) are inevitably called into question by the oppressed, if not by the oppressors themselves. Their very status as oppressors and their loyalty to the goals, objectives, and processes of marginalization raise the distinct possibility that none of their actions are free from a sort of social original sin. Thus one must wonder how moral responsibility can be exercised by either the oppressor or the oppressed in a situation of oppression. For the purposes of this inquiry we assume that in many respects the oppressed have acted in a morally responsible fashion. And it must be further assumed that, on occasion, even oppressors, acting among themselves, are effective moral agents.[4] How does marginalization feel? Of what does it really consist? These questions may be answered only by hearing the oppressed.

The problems of marginalized people are well described by a liberation theologian, Julio De Santa Ana. De Santa Ana recalls a conversation with the oppressed of Uruguay:

"Why do you people defecate all around here: Don't you know it's bad for your health?" "Mister, you'd do the same if you had one lavatory a furlong away for 500 people!" In a family planning session in a village a woman talks: "You ask me to limit my family. But I need children, more children, see? They are the ones who help me with the family income. If I want three children to remain alive, I have to produce at least ten." She is right. She lost many children and she speaks from experience. Her children start working at the age of 5. Some roll incense sticks (bidis) or local leaf cigarettes, some are in road gangs pouring hot tar on crushed stones all through the hot day. For these children, there is no such thing as childhood. Everyday life is a continuous anguish for this family, not knowing where they are to live, when they will eat next . . . "I do not bathe for months," brags the man who gets his pittance as a labourer. "I work the whole day in the hot sun and I need water to wash myself. In this slum we had water before but now it belongs to the landlord who has taken over the place. Who can afford a bath if you have to pay for every pot of water?" A woman, after a lifetime of labour in the tea gardens, dies, and is buried in the tea gardens in a cask made out of tea chests. Over her grave will grow bushes of tea, whose leaves will refresh many. . . . In life and in death, people like her could never hope for an identity that befits a human being.[5]

Clearly, the task of the responsible self in a marginalized community is to join the oppressed in the struggle to transform the world within the midst of an existential experience of marginalization. We reaffirm our humanity when we affirm co-marginalists. As Gustavo Gutiérrez puts it, our task is a difficult one:

> This is why our question is not how to speak of God in an adult world. That was the old question asked by progressivist theology. No, the interlocutor of the theology of liberation is the "nonperson," the human being who is not considered human by the present social or-der—the exploited classes, marginalized ethnic groups, and despised cultures. Our question is how to tell the nonperson, the nonhuman, that God is love, and that this love makes us all brothers and sisters.[6]

A noted African-American ethicist, Katie Cannon, further describes the conditions of oppression and brutalization of black women, the group of people in America that is probably most marginalized. Cannon writes:

> According to the various sex and race groups, Black women still earn the least. Abbey Lincoln demythologizes the Black woman's social progress in her cryptic depiction of the contemporary Black woman. "Her head is more regularly beaten than any other woman's, and by her own man; she's the scapegoat for Mr. Charlie; she is forced to stark realism and chided if caught dreaming; her aspirations for her and hers are, for sanity's sake, stunted; her physical image has been crimi-nally maligned, assaulted, and negated; she is the first to be called ugly, and never yet beautiful.[7]

Cannon's unflinching look at the condition of African-American women reminds us that oppression is not the sole responsibility of one race (black men are oppressively involved in her depiction), sex (elsewhere in her work, white women are cited as oppressors), or class. The condition of oppression often creates a peculiar perspective and consciousness. Mem-bership in societies plagued with oppression always has a distinctly odd flavor. Either it is experienced as insufficiently secured, in the same way that a nonoppressed membership regulates the membership of its children, or it is experienced as fully realized but subject to sudden, unpredictable collapses.

In the first instance, marginalized membership is experienced as some-thing akin to an imposed childhood. For lack of a better term, this form of oppression may be called infantilization. It is experienced by marginalized people so beset by some or all of the aspects of their marginality that they are seldom able to exercise fully their moral agency in realizing any of their life plans, and, with regard to their needs, they are often prevented from engaging in the necessary political discourse that goes on in their societies. Like the children of nonoppressed members of their society, these folks experience a certain kind of paternalistic recognition, but their basic moral capacity is never fully acknowledged by the community of oppression. In contrast, the latter membership problem, or experience of oppression, consists of a kind of sustainable marginality. It is the experience faced by people such as this writer, people who are not necessarily poor or economically deprived, who are often successful in their careers, but are oppressed, nevertheless, because their belonging to a hated or traditionally subjugated ethnic or religious group subjects them to sudden, drastic, destabilizing acts of oppression. Such "members" of society feel reasonably secure until an incident of police brutality or a lynching occurs to remind us that we skate on the thin ice of a hostile society and are subject to sudden, fatal plunges into unseen, unanticipated fissures in the frozen depths of white supremacy.[8] Thus when the oppressed and oppressors engage in an interaction, how is responsible action manifested? This question must now be explored because it was not adequately addressed by Niebuhr.

Assuming that at least some marginalized people are morally responsible, is their approach superior or inferior to Niebuhr's approach? To answer this question requires a careful application of Niebuhr's categories of moral reasoning, and also of ethical reflection, to the practices of marginalized people. To accomplish this preliminary task requires an initial analysis of Niebuhr's approach that looks at the self's understanding of its own security and its understanding of its own perspective; examines Niebuhr's phenomenological epistemology; analyzes important aspects of moral reasoning such as accountability, and social solidarity; and, finally, analyzes Niebuhr's Christology. The subsequent comparison with marginalized responsibilists comprises several steps: first, a characterization of marginalized people; second, a comparison of primary categories of moral reasoning and certain characteristic responses of the marginalized; and third, an examination of a proposed Christology deemed appropriate for the marginalized that is diametrically opposed to Niebuhr's Christology.

Finally, we compare liberationist approaches and Niebuhr's approach to discover the primary problem with current responsibilist ethics and to set the stage for the formal critical examination of the lives and practices of carefully selected marginalized responsibilists and how they actually reflected and acted in their communities.

The introduction concludes with a complete explanation of the structure of this book, the methodology to be used, and a brief historical examination of one moral exemplar that reveals a new responsibilist understanding of moral agency and the will of God in liberating and sustaining humanity. This examination suggests that from a moral point of view, marginalized people are not on the margins of moral reasoning and ethical living, but rather at their center. We are kept at the center, at least in part, not simply by our own efforts in moral living, but also by oppressors, whose acts of oppression force us to the moral center of human interaction while they simultaneously force themselves to the margins of ethical living. This process of moral inversion is an unintended side effect of oppression; that is to say, oppressors do not intend to dehumanize themselves when they oppress others, although that is the inevitable consequence of their actions.[9]

A COMPARISON OF RESPONSIBLE SELVES: STRUCTURE AND METHODOLOGY

Our review of responsible marginalists will show that God has a preferential option for the poor and oppressed that needs to be recognized by the marginalized and by empowered allies who wish to stand in solidarity with us.[10] This recognition constitutes a new disposition that is established firmly in the marginalized as a response to our oppression. It is manifested in our interpretation of the Bible and is itself, at the minimum, consistent with Niebuhr's approach.[11]

A brief outline of Niebuhr's explanation of moral reasoning for responsible selves constitutes the structure of this book. Each moral exemplar will be analyzed as if he/she were a responsible self. How each understood the divine initiative, basic response, interpretation, accountability, and social solidarity will be analyzed to see, in part, whether or not some of the distinctions between *homo dialogicus* (dialogical humanity) and *homo dialogicus marginalis* (marginalized dialogical humanity) are discernible in his/her life and work. Of course, the analysis will note carefully how each marginalist responded to the two communities, that of the oppressed and that of the oppressors. Throughout the book, Niebuhr's pattern will continue to provide the structure, including his understanding of several important issues: the interpretation of history; God's will for the world; Christ's place and function in this scheme; and the moral ramifications of these concepts.

The responsible selves chosen for this study are Bishop Henry McNeal Turner (1834–1915), Ida B. Wells-Barnett (1869–1931), and Rev. Francis J. Grimké (1850–1937). These figures were marginalized leaders in oppressed communities. Their ethical reasoning and praxis as responsible selves located in marginalized communities serve as practical guidelines for understanding how morally responsible people act in situations of oppression. All of these persons were roughly contemporaneous, and all predated H. Richard Niebuhr. That they predate Niebuhr is important because their approaches to moral reasoning and their ethical praxis, along with those of other marginalized selves, were available to Niebuhr and other moral theorists of his era.

Chapter 2 examines the earliest figure, Bishop Henry McNeal Turner. Chapter 3 turns to Mrs. Ida B. Wells-Barnett, and Chapter 4 to Rev. Francis J. Grimké. Chapter 5 compares the three figures and shows that the marginalized have an ethic of responsibility that encompasses a variety of responses to oppression and other problems. In so doing, this chapter demonstrates that marginalized people can successfully lead moral Christian lives and, in fact, can serve as moral exemplars for nonmarginalized people. Furthermore, the paradigm for resistance to oppression, as characterized in particular by the quest to meet basic needs in solidarity with the poor and oppressed, and the struggle for liberation are both shown to be aspects of God's ongoing project for the salvation and the reconciliation of humanity.[12]

Chapter 6 sums up the arguments presented and demonstrates that the duties of the poor and the oppressed and the project of God are the joint obligations of all Christians as well as of others who are committed to the struggle for justice and sustainability. This book concludes, accordingly, with a discussion of the variety of international duties that may be created by the fulfillment of such a vision and the inherent limitations to this approach.

Although the limits of this work will not permit a wider review of sources, or a detailed blueprint for conducting oneself as a responsible self in relation to God and others in a marginalized community, it should be noted that similar approaches are also discernible in David Walker, Henry Highland Garnett, Sojourner Truth, Frederick Douglass, and many others.[13] For the most part, however, these responsible selves were not heard by contemporary nonmarginalized interpreters of morality. The understanding of the oppressed and their attempts at living the Christian moral life were ignored in favor of the patterns and practices of the ruling majorities or their traditional religious and ethical interpreters. This practice of systematic distortion of communication flourishes even at this moment and is part of the tragedy of oppression, in which, to borrow Paulo Freire's language, the inhabitants of a culture of silence are not made mute but are systematically ignored.[14] In a similar fashion, the responsible selves featured herein have also been ignored. Their understanding of Christian moral responsibility is not, therefore, derived from Niebuhr's work but may best be understood when compared to his work. Rather than attempt to impose a revisionist order on their work that they never intended, it is better to examine and interpret their work and thought according to the categories that Niebuhr has suggested.

Technically, *The Responsible Self* is not a book on Christian ethics but rather a prolegomenon to Christian ethics. As such, it is Niebuhr's attempt to develop a typology of moral experience. It is therefore only an initial attempt to interpret human responsibility in a pluralist world that has many attractive groups, each competing for our loyalty and our devotion.[15] Niebuhr forces us to ask a series of timeless questions: (1) To whom (or what) am I responsible? (2) For whom (or what) am I responsible? (3) To what moral community do I belong? These are relational questions that every individual asks in the course of a lifetime.[16] The groups to which we belong give us answers to these questions; at the same time they require us to respond with support, criticism, and, on occasion, submission.

The following work represents an attempt to fill in some of the blanks left by Niebuhr in the *Responsible Self*.[17] Yet in filling in the blanks, contradictions to his work must be anticipated because of several factors: (1) the passage of time; (2) the influence of other voices in the ethical conversation; and, most important, (3) the different perspectives, community ties, and interests of the authors.

Chapter 1

The "Responsible Self": Who Is He/She?

H. Richard Niebuhr's biography is too well known to require a reexamination. Suffice it to say that as a first-generation American, the bilingual son of a noted German immigrant, theologian/pastor of the German Evangelical Synod of North America, a product of the well-educated and cultured middle class, a college and seminary graduate, Niebuhr was not a member of what William J. Wilson, a prominent sociologist, has designated as the "truly disadvantaged."[1] This is not to say that Niebuhr never experienced hardships, defeats, or depressions. James Fowler's *To See the Kingdom* details some of the struggles that Niebuhr faced, which were sufficiently severe to cause him to be hospitalized for a brief period of time.[2] However, Niebuhr was never located in a marginalized community. He wrote out of his experience as a moral agent in a nonmarginalized community. From early on in his career, he was a partisan of marginalized people.[3] Yet he himself was never trapped in an individual or group situation in which his humanity was constantly questioned and in which his survival was severely challenged by powerful opponents. Niebuhr's own call to ethical action reveals the basic sustainability of his subject:

> Yet in one sense we must go farther, and arrive at a conclusion. This farther step cannot be taken on the plane of understanding, and this conclusion cannot be reached in the realm of theoretic insight and outlook. They are undertaken and attained in the movement from consideration to action, from insight to decision. Each believer reaches

his [sic] own "final" conclusion, in resolutions that involve a leap from the chair in which he has read about ancient battles into the middle of a present conflict. No amount of speculative insight into the consideration of the imperatives and values issuing from Christ and culture, can relieve the Christian individual or the responsible Christian community from the burden, the necessity, the guilt and glory, of arriving at such conclusions in present decisions and present obedience.[4]

Obviously, Niebuhr's ethical protagonist is not an armchair dilettante; yet he also is not in any immediate danger of extermination, nor is he constantly subjected to systemic oppression because of considerations of race, gender, or class.

NIEBUHR'S PHENOMENOLOGY

Niebuhr's empowered self begins ethical reflection with a focus on human moral experience, the human moral life in general.[5] For Niebuhr the first question is, "What is going on?" If his approach is viable and applicable to universal human moral experience, it should also be illuminative for marginalized people. Indeed, Niebuhr's epistemological commitment to human experience invites a comparison of various class, race, and gender experiences. Niebuhr's primary root metaphor for humanity is homo dialogicus—humanity as responder to prior action and communication.[6] He preferred his moral agent to two older types, namely *homo faber* (humanity-as-makers) and *homo politicus* (humanity-as-citizens).[7] He prefers the homo dialogicus to the other types because, in part, he understands all human action as being predicated upon the prior action of God. Thus *all* human action is action of response; homo dialogicus is, therefore, the most adequate and comprehensive description of moral agency. As Niebuhr suggests, how people are to interpret all actions upon them as being the action of God is very important and highly problematic. However, for the present, attention to this problem must be postponed.

Even for Niebuhr, however, not all the action that humans experience comes directly from God, for he understood that society also acts as a primary shaper of individual conscience, virtues, habits, and actions. In addition, humans constantly interact with nature. Thus the actions of individuals are always in response to God, or to others, or to nature. Two important conclusions can be drawn with regard to the self, according to Niebuhr. First, the self is never an atomistic individual unrelated to society.[8] Second, human response is the primary Niebuhrian category that will serve as a point of inquiry in each of our moral exemplars. To distinguish between mere response and responsibility, Niebuhr introduces the concept of interpretation.

INTERPRETATION OF ACTION AND HISTORIES

Humans are interpretive beings, and the nature and quality of a human response is predicated upon the individual or group interpretation of prior action.[9] Niebuhr understands the self as being a "timefull" self:

> Yet the phenomenal self I know in being known, the selves my companions reveal to me, the self that knows itself as it acts, defines, decides, chooses, or otherwise moves out from itself, is timefull in ways of which teleology and deontology seem unaware. It is a self that is always in the present to be sure, always in the moment, so that the very notion of the present is probably unthinkable apart from some implicit reference to a self. I and now belong together somewhat as do I and Thou and I and It do. . . . My past is with me now; it is in my present as conscious and unconscious memory; it is here now as habit of behavior, of speech and thought, as ways of cutting up and dividing into shapes and forms the great mass of impressions made on my senses by the energies assailing them from without. My interpersonal past also is with me in all my present meetings with other selves. It is there in all my love and guilt. The self does not leave its past behind as the moving hand of a clock does; its past is inscribed into it more deeply than the past of geologic formations is crystallized in their present form.[10]

Clearly, Niebuhr was aware of an oppressive past and what such a past might mean to present selves. Of such a past he noted:

> We do not destroy this past of ours; it is indestructible. We carry it with us; its record is written deep into our lives. We only refuse to acknowledge it as our true past and try to make it an alien thing— something that did not happen to our real selves. So our national histories do not recall to the consciousness of citizens the crimes and absurdities of past social conduct, as our written and unwritten autobiographies fail to mention our shame. But this unremembered past endures. An external view can see its embodiment in the boundaries of nations, in the economic status of groups, such as that of Negroes in America, in folkways and customs whose origins have been forgotten, in national policies and in personal habits. When we live and act in accordance with our inward social constitution in which there are class and race divisions, prejudices, assumptions about the

things we can and cannot do, we are constrained by the unconscious past.[11]

These long passages reveal Niebuhr's guilt with regard to the oppressive American past history of subjugating African Americans, among others. Full repentance for such a past and the creation of new relationships required, for him, a reinterpretation of that past:

> Insofar as the reinterpretation of our past has led us to some new understanding and acceptance of the past actions of and upon our groups, our present encounters with each other as North and South, Negro and white, have been guided by somewhat new ideas. Every nation with similar social recollections of past animosities, with a similar inherited complex of emotional and personal attitudes of group to group, seeks, I believe, to move toward freedom, toward freshness and fittingness in present interaction by similar reconstructions of its past.[12]

This willingness to recognize the reality of oppression in past actions and the indestructibility of the past and its ability to influence present and future relationships indicates, logically, that Niebuhr should find that a predisposition to be in solidarity with the oppressed is a fitting response in most situations. Thus the liberationist predilection for favoring the poor and oppressed, if not an extension of Niebuhr's thought, is not ruled out by it either.[13] Yet it must be said that a willingness to accept a reinterpretation of a common internal history is not the same as the ready ability to perform such an act of reinterpretation.

ACCOUNTABILITY AND SOCIAL SOLIDARITY FOR THE EMPOWERED SELF

The third element in Niebuhr's process of moral reasoning centers on the concept of accountability. Niebuhr understood accountability to consist in the ongoing action of an ethical agent in which the agent's actions occur after interpretation and reflection, but in which he/she also holds himself/herself available to accept the consequences of the action.[14] The concept of accountability naturally entails the concept of a society that can hold an individual accountable and that can be held accountable in a similar fashion by its members. This recognition of the absolute concreteness of society again emphasizes the social nature of Niebuhr's concept of the self. His concept of accountability posits a society that converses and interacts with each moral agent.

In contrast, the marginalized self invariably has at least two societies that must be related to responsibly.[15] As will be elaborated on in a later section, homo dialogicus marginalis, the responsible self in the marginalized community, has two dialogue partners; one consists of his/her oppressed siblings and the other consists of the society of oppressors. Yet the oppressed's conversation with the oppressor is always a form of systematically distorted communication, in which oppressors are invariably predisposed to hear what they want to hear, and the oppressed are invariably constrained to strategically structure their communications with ruthless power so as to minimize the punishments and threats inherent in this interchange.[16] The object of this careful calculation is to make oneself heard without surrendering any material, spiritual, or psychological advantages already realized in prior interrelations. The morally responsible person of the marginalized community also seeks to preserve his/her self-esteem, which sometimes requires him/her to risk punishment by making comments that are likely to displease the powerful.

Thus the issue of accountability also highlights the differences in response of the two types of selves. Homo dialogicus, as an empowered yet limited self, must be accountable to his/her nonmarginalized community and to God. It is not clear, however, how she/he is also accountable to the oppressed. Niebuhr himself was horrified at the "color line" in American Christianity.[17] With regard to the use of the historic slave gallery, he revealed an awareness of the ability of at least some marginalized people to resist oppression:

> The slave gallery was as much of an institution in the house of God as in the theater. It had its uses, to be sure, and its defenders among Negroes as well as among the whites. Yet it was a badge of white superiority and of colored inferiority before the throne of God; against it awakened Negroes could not but rebel.[18]

Although sensitive to the discrimination that blacks of his own era experienced, Niebuhr was nevertheless culturally ignorant and biased with regard to African-American Christianity. He interpreted the "liveliness" of the black religion of his generation as simply betokening a lack of education and an absence of high culture.[19] Thus he recognized the existence of oppressed people in his world but was unable to be fully accountable to them. Most of this problem can be attributed to the inherently distorted patterns of communication and ambiguous social status determinations that are inevitably found in relations between oppressors and the oppressed. It is seldom clear to the oppressed or oppressors whether or not, and to what extent, if any, the oppressed are members of society. Clearly, we are second-class citizens whose membership is less than full or we could not rightly regard ourselves as oppressed. Yet in some respects, oppressor and oppressed find themselves in covenant with each other. Perhaps this confused inter-relationship explains Niebuhr's own praxeological stance in regard to social solidarity, his last important consideration in moral reasoning. When this approach is compared to liberationist approaches, we find that Niebuhr recognized the segregation of his era (which was a form of oppression) but did not see that the fitting response would be for segregationists to integrate with the oppressed.[20] For Niebuhr, the responsible self understood itself to be completely embedded in its society, but this understanding did not, as a general rule, oblige him/her to side with the oppressed, or even to communicate sufficiently with the oppressed to gain insight into their perspective.

To summarize, Niebuhr's responsible self is a socialized self, an im-perfect rather than the ideal one. It is not perfectly objective; it is not a nous, floating above the world of concerns. It is not the artificial self of the social contract, the risk-aversive calculator of interests that drives much of liberal political economic theory. Nor is this self the fundamentalist self, confident that the Bible is the clear repository of God's word and wisdom and that she or he, the special agent of the Holy Spirit, is faithfully and unerringly working in the world. Yet this homo dialogicus is not a homo dialogicus marginalis. In exercising moral agency, this self does not lead a disgraced and tenuous existence. Furthermore, Niebuhr's homo dialogicus does not face the psychological and spiritual struggles of the marginalis variety. Yet to fully understand Niebuhr' approach, we must examine his Christology.

THE RESPONSIBLE CHRIST OF THE EMPOWERED SELF

Niebuhr rejects the Barthian notion that Christian theology can be understood exclusively by means of Christological analogies, metaphors, or symbols.[21] He realizes that in order to understand Jesus Christ, a Christian must interpret the symbols, metaphors, analogies, and stories in the Bible in relation to Christ and in relation to Christ's relationship with God. E. Clinton Gardner, in particular, is correct in maintaining that Niebuhr was primarily theocentric rather than Christocentric.[22] Nevertheless, Niebuhr understood Jesus Christ to be the primary revelation of God:

> The God who reveals himself in Jesus Christ is now trusted and known as the contemporary God, revealing himself in every event; but we do not understand how we could trace his working in these hap-penings if he did not make himself known to us through the memory of Jesus Christ; nor do we know how we should be able to interpret all the words we read as words of God save by the aid of this Rosetta stone.[23]

Thus Niebuhr maintained that Christians know God, at least in part, through the memory of, and in relationship with, Jesus Christ. But Jesus has a dual function and orientation.[24] He reveals God to humanity but also serves as a symbol of self-understanding and moral action:

> The situation of Christians then seems to be this: they cannot understand themselves or direct their actions or give form to their conduct without the use of the symbol Jesus Christ, but with the aid of that symbol only they never succeed in understanding themselves and their values or in giving shape to their conduct.[25]

Although Niebuhr studiously avoids espousing an ethic that requires believers to simply emulate Jesus, he nevertheless sees Christ as the moral exemplar par excellence; that is to say, Niebuhr finds in Christ the perfect homo dialogicus, the human who interprets all action upon himself as being the action of God, and who then, as the Son of God, makes the appropriate response:

> First of all, he is the responsible man who in all his responses to alterations did what fitted into the divine action. He interpreted every alteration that he encountered as a sign of the action of God, of the universal omnificent one, whom he called Father. He responded to all action upon him as one who anticipated the divine answer to his answers. Will of God meant for him not only or primarily divine imperative but the divine action, carried out through many agencies besides those of men obedient to commandment.[26]

According to this interpretation of Christ, Jesus expresses ultimate loyalty to God through the crucifixion. However, Jesus' loyalty and obedience are correspondingly shown to be justified in God's resurrection of Jesus. Yet the Jesus of Nazareth that Niebuhr looks to is not a Jesus as revolutionary liberator, but rather a loyal, trusting, sacrificial Son of God. This Jesus does not display a revolutionary praxis on behalf of the marginalized that directly challenges the status quo:

> The strategy of Jesus, the Jewish revolutionary, centers in the principles of repentance, faith, forgiveness and innocence suffering for guilt. It is impossible for man to take the Kingdom by violence, by self-assertion; he has no means adequate to this purpose. But it is possible for him, in repentance, to anticipate the judgment, to give up the attempt to reserve or extend the dying system and so to hasten its destruction.[27]

Niebuhr's Jesus does not engage in confrontational practices that further human liberation in order for Christians to reflect upon or to emulate them; instead, this Jesus has a certain humility and is inclined to suffer for God's reign. Since, as we will see, our marginalists and modern liberationists have very different characterizations of Jesus, it is not unfair to state that no reasonable reading of H. R. Niebuhr's work would classify it as an explicit form of liberation ethics.[28] That this is a reliable conclusion may be seen by the absence in the work of liberationist language with reference to Jesus and others. In addition, in contrast to nearly all liberation theologians and ethicists, Niebuhr maintains that God moves in ways that dictate the chastising of people by oppression *in conformance* with the will of God. For Niebuhr, the will of God is generous and ineluctable:

> The will of God is what God does in all that nature and men do.
> It is the universal that contains and transforms, includes and fashions,
> every particular. Will of God is present for Jesus in every event from
> the death of sparrows, the shining of sun and descent of rain, through
> the exercise of authority by ecclesiastical and political powers that
> abuse their authority, through treachery and desertion by disciples,
> to the impending beleaguerment of Jerusalem and the end of an aeon.
> . . . His action is more like that of the great wise leader who uses even
> the meannesses of his subjects to promote the public welfare.[29]

Thus the evil of oppressors may be interpreted by modern Niebuhrian scholars to be a working out of God's infinite design rather than an act of idolatry that should be resisted. God cannot be said, from this point of view, to have an irrevocable commitment to the project of human liberation by means, in part, of moral agents who, as servants of God, resist oppression and relieve the suffering of the oppressed.[30] Niebuhr's God, then, is not a God of liberation. Thus we arrive at a central question: can a general predisposition to solidarity with the poor and oppressed—which is common to liberation theologians—be applied to Niebuhr's approach without distorting that approach and constituting thereby a departure from his approach? If it cannot, then the liberationist must choose between continuing to employ Niebuhr's approach or abandoning it in order to promote the struggle for liberation. Furthermore, this choice would mean that a liberation theologian would have to abandon Niebuhr's legacy because it is enmeshed in oppression and constitutes an obstacle to liberation ethics rather than a resource for liberation-oriented moral reasoning. To help settle this question, it is useful to compare Niebuhr's understanding of the self with the way marginalized selves understand themselves and how they act, a task to which our attention now turns.

THE MARGINALIZED MORALITY OF THE CHALLENGED SELF:
A DIFFERENT RESPONSE, INTERPRETATION, AND ACCOUNTABILITY

An examination of W. E. B. Du Bois' description of an African-American version of the self further helps to distinguish between Niebuhr's protagonist and that of the oppressed self. The marginalized self has a "double consciousness." Du Bois' description of this phenomenon is still striking and timeless:

> Here, then, is the dilemma, and it is a puzzling one, I admit. No Negro who has given earnest thought to the situation of his people in America has failed, at some time in life, to find himself at these crossroads; has failed to ask himself at some time; what, after all am I? Am I an American or am I a Negro? Can I be both? Or is it my duty to cease to be a Negro as soon as possible and be an American? It is such incessant *self-questioning* and the hesitation that arises from it, that is making the present period a time of vacillation and contradiction for the American Negro. . . . Here, it seems to me, is the reading of the riddle that puzzles so many of us. We are Americans, not only by birth and by citizenship, but by our political ideals, our language, our religion. Farther than that, our Americanism does not go. At that point, we are Negroes, members of a vast historic race that from the very dawn of creation has slept, but half awakening in the dark forests of its African fatherland. We are the first fruits of this new nation, the harbinger of that black tomorrow which is yet destined to soften the whiteness of the Teutonic today. We are that people whose subtle sense of song has given America its only American music, its only American fairy tales, its only touch of pathos and humor amid its mad money-getting plutocracy.[31]

Elsewhere Du Bois wrote:

> One ever feels his twoness—An American, a Negro; two souls, two thoughts, two unreconciled strivings; two warring ideals in one dark body, whose dogged strength alone keeps it from being torn asunder. The history of the American Negro is the history of this strife,—this longing to attain *self-conscious manhood*, to merge his *double self* into a better and truer self.[32]

Du Bois' famous description of double consciousness reveals more than the psychological stresses that oppressed African Americans often feel. It also reveals the two societies that marginalized people are obliged to deal with: the society of the oppressed as a society of open membership that is embedded in a second society, that of oppression. In comparison, Niebuhr's closest association with the world of oppression may be found in his discussion of the problem of suffering caused by the reality of evil. The problem of resisting evil was apparent to Niebuhr, who well understood that suffering was a reality for much of humanity. Indeed, the following excerpt shows he understood how the response(s) of individuals and groups actively shape and define individuals and groups: "Yet it is in the response to suffering that many and perhaps all men, individually and in their groups, define themselves, take on character, develop their ethos. And their responses are functions of their interpretation of what is happening to them as well as of the action upon them."[33]

This recognition of the relationship between adversity and group and individual character formation is a strength in Niebuhr's approach. Of course, the term *suffering* is not synonymous with the term *oppression;* instead, it is a description of one of the actual experiences that the oppressed feel.[34] Although Niebuhr insightfully noted the former term, he did not explore the latter one. Thus when Niebuhr's self begins its moral inquiry, it does so with the rather innocent question, "What is going on?"[35] Niebuhr's question is not purely egocentric. In asking it, he is asking about every discernible event: human history, interdependence, and social exchanges. Because of Niebuhr's approach to ethics, his question leads naturally to theological inquiries. This sustainable self's task of interpretation is complex. She/he has a variety of experiences, many of which are pleasant. In a similar fashion, the responsible self has all of the same concerns. But, in addition, the truly marginalized person must also ask, "Besides my ongoing experience of being oppressed, in a marginalized community, what else is going on?" This additional, slightly different question makes an enormous phenomenological difference in how the respective selves engage in ethical reflection.

James Cone maintains that moral inquiry by the oppressed begins with the recognition of the experience of oppression. With regard to the marginalized self's concept of freedom, he writes:

> It is not difficult for the oppressed to understand the meaning of freedom. They are forced by the very nature of their condition to interpret their existence in the world contrary to the value-structures of an oppressive society. For the oppressed, to be is to be in revolt against the forces that impede the creation of the new person.[36]

In short, homo dialogicus marginalis is constrained to understand existence in society itself as an ongoing challenge. In contrast, Niebuhr's self, as one that is obliged to rise from his or her armchair to go forth and meet sudden, occasional perils in life, has a substantially different perspective.

One of Niebuhr's greatest contributions to social ethics, however, was his recognition and acknowledgment of the unavoidable historical, cultural, social, and political relativity of all ethical reflection.[37] Yet, writing prior to the advent of liberation theology—prior to James Cone, José Míguez Bonino, Jacquelyn Grant, and Gustavo Gutiérrez, among others—Niebuhr retains an inquiring "socialized" self that does not see its basic integrity as being immediately and constantly called into question. Its possible courses of action begin to be considered from a perspective that understands itself and its world as essentially free and sustainable. The marginalized self has no such luxury.

Accordingly, the responsible self in a marginalized community performs Niebuhr's second categorical act of moral reasoning, that of interpretation, differently. Experiencing a different reality than that of homo dialogicus, homo dialogicus marginalis interprets the actions of society and God differently. The microsociety of the oppressed may well be analogous to Niebuhr's original notion of society, but the macrosociety of oppression is understood by the oppressed as being hostile and evil. As James Cone has made clear, the oppressed interpret past and present actions and anticipate future actions with the awareness of the pain of oppression.[38]

At this point homo dialogicus marginalis has a perspectival advantage over the empowered self, since he or she is much less inclined to rationalize and reify an oppressive past. The ongoing experience of victimization also inclines him or her to actively reinterpret the past so that the present and future may be altered and relief from oppression may become a reality rather than a fond eschatological hope. Again, James Cone graphically illustrates the superior interpretive ability of the oppressed on this point, in comparison with the ability of oppressors. With regard to the diminished interpretive ability of oppressive whites, he writes:

This is not to deny that whites are enslaved. What we deny is their ability to know and analyze their slavery. The depravity of oppressors is their enslavement to their own "freedom." Because they are free to do what they will to the oppressed, the only check being their pious feelings about the world, it is not possible for them to see the oppressed as human beings. The oppressed become objects to be used to make the world more amenable to the whims of the masters. Thus oppressors are enslaved and dehumanized by their own will to power. They storm the citadel of the gods, claiming sole authority to declare what is real and right, and to shape the world accordingly. If they are to be liberated from such megalomania, it must be done by the oppressed. When the oppressed affirm their freedom by refusing to behave according to the master's rules, they not only liberate themselves from oppression, but they also liberate oppressors from enslavement to their illusions. The basic error of white comments about their own oppression is the assumption that they *know* the nature of their enslavement. This cannot be so, because if they really knew, they would liberate themselves by joining the revolution of the black community.[39]

Thus it is to homo dialogicus marginalis that the aware homo dialogicus must turn for at least the preliminary stages of reinterpretation and recreation of social relationships.[40] This is why our review of the lives of marginalized responsibilists is integral to a reinterpretation and reformulation of responsibilist ethics. These marginalists reinterpret God, human response, accountability, and social solidarity in ways that permit a critical reinterpretation of the past that does not doom people to the moral redundancy of simply repeating past acts of oppression in new and even more perverse forms. And the foremost reinterpretation for liberationists and marginalists centers not merely on a reinterpretation of themselves, or their oppressors, or whatever common history they share, but often instead on the soteriological plan of God and the role of Christ in that project.

THE RESPONSIBLE CHRIST: GOD'S AGENT OF LIBERATION

James Cone distinguishes the liberationist position from Niebuhr's position by declaring that God intentionally wills the liberation of the oppressed and that Jesus is God's foremost agent of liberation:

> Despite the emphasis on future redemption in present suffering, black theology cannot accept any view of God that even indirectly places divine approval on human suffering. The death and resurrection of Jesus does not mean that God promises us a future reality in order that we might tolerate present evil. The suffering that Jesus accepted and which is promised to his disciples is not to be equated with the easy acceptance of human injustice inflicted by white oppressors. God cannot be the God of blacks and will their suffering. To be elected by God does not mean freely accepting the evils of oppressors. The suffering which is inseparable from the gospel is that style of existence that arises from a decision to be in spite of nonbeing. . . . Providence, then, is not a statement about the future. It does not mean that all things will work out for the best for those who love God. Providence is a statement about present reality—the reality of the liberation of the oppressed.[41]

Cone goes on to say:

> Blacks cannot adhere to a view of God that will weaken their drive for liberation. This means that in a racist society, we must insist that God's love and God's righteousness are two ways of talking about the same reality. Righteousness means that God is addressing the black condition; love means that God is doing so in the interests of both blacks and whites.[42]

Thus for Cone, God's will is committed to a justice that is partisan for the powerless: God intends for humans to be free and whole, and this is God's project, not merely the project of the underclass. In contrast, for Niebuhr, the will of God is far more opaque. Consequently, Cone is critical of Niebuhr's understanding of Jesus Christ and the project of God:

> He [Niebuhr] is right in stressing the *dialectical* relations of love, hope, obedience, faith, and humility as these virtues are particularized in Jesus' person, but he does not go far enough. Indeed, it can be said that what Niebuhr says about Christ is incorrect not so much in terms of what he says but in terms of what he fails to say. This absence is so crucial to the biblical picture of Christ that without it the biblical Christ no longer exists. I am referring to Jesus' identity with the little ones and his proclamation that God wills their freedom. If we are to accept the biblical revelation as the point of departure for a picture of Christ, then we must ask whether it is possible to talk about Christ in any sense without making his identity with the oppressed the starting point? I think not. . . . The biblical Christ is primarily the Liberator of the oppressed from human bondage. He is God's revelation who has come to set the captives free. Therefore, whatever is said about love, hope, obedience, faith, and humility in Christ must be interpreted in the light of his identity with the poor for the purpose of their liberation. While Niebuhr does not exclude Christ's identity with the poor, they nonetheless are not the point of departure of his christological perspective.[43]

Obviously, Cone is more openly Christological than Niebuhr. However, his criticism of Niebuhr is not that he is too theocentric; rather, Cone finds that his Christology is fatally incomplete. Furthermore, Niebuhr's God is too ambivalent with regard to the plight of the oppressed. For Cone, Jesus is more of a liberator than a comforter. Yet what is not clear from reading Cone is whether his understanding of Jesus constitutes what marginalized people should believe about Christ or is instead a description of what they actually believe. Our case studies will demonstrate that marginalized people have a variety of views on Jesus Christ, as well as the scope and intent of their soteriology.

What this last discussion means for responsibilist ethics is quite important. Niebuhr's position implies that it may be ethically justifiable for marginalized people to simply acquiesce in the process of their marginalization, and for empowered responsible selves to refrain from intervening in the conflicts of the world.[44] E. Clinton Gardner asserts that Niebuhr's refusal to unqualifiedly pronounce a project as being of God is essential to his method:

> On the one hand, an ethics of responsibility (as the primary model) must necessarily resist the effort to give the will or action of God any unqualified specificity. To do otherwise would be to substitute an abstract conception of value/duty for a relational one; it would be to absolutize a human perception of value when there is no absolute except the will of God.[45]

It is to this precise point that this book responds. An insightful and reliable commentator on Niebuhr's work, Gardner correctly interprets Niebuhr's intent and motivations, but he fails fully to appreciate, as did Niebuhr, the fullest implications of a responsibilist ethic. The rationale for this conclusion is fairly simple. Since the responsible self is required to interpret the prior action of God, co-humanity, and nature, such a self is entitled to interpret the action of God, through Jesus Christ, as a redemption that includes a liberation from spiritual sin and the structures of oppression erected by sin. It might be concluded, through this interpretation, that such sin encourages further acts of sin, nurtures present relationships predicated on sin, and enmeshes future relationships—individually, in institutions, and in groups—in expressions of sin, such sin being that of oppression.

To break this cycle, the marginalized might well recognize that the divine initiative of God opposes structural oppression as it does any other form of evil. Since Niebuhr does understand that God opposes evil, even from his perspective a fitting response to evil would be to oppose it because it is one of the many idols that masquerade as the highest value that can be found only in relationship with the One beyond the Many. Thus it does not contradict the most fully realized implications of Niebuhr's work to say that the project of God entails the liberation of men and women from the chains that oppressors and the oppressed wear and impose on each other. Such a response to the divine initiative, even if strategically incorrect, is a responsible response to the prior action of God, and a reasonable interpretation for the marginalized to have discovered and discerned. Therefore the adoption of a preferential option for the poor, which goes hand in hand with the conception of God as liberator, is a reasonable extension of Niebuhr's understanding of social solidarity and universal loyalty.[46] The responsible self could say with confidence that God is a God of liberation with a preferential option for the poor, knowing full well that her or his interpretation, although it is socially, culturally, historically, and economically relative, nevertheless constitutes a fitting response.[47] The concept of Jesus as Liberator does not contradict the concept of Jesus as redeemer that is already present in the Niebuhrian corpus, except that the role is an extension of Niebuhr's understanding of Christ's and God's intentions. This is not to say, however, that Niebuhr had this approach. However, if Christ is interpreted as being a liberator as well as a redeemer, then the followers of Christ, while perhaps not slavishly following Christ's example as liberator, must nevertheless be opposed to oppression and open to the possibility of being used by God to transform the world and to oppose oppression while simultaneously supporting freedom, opportunity, and equality. A responsible self might not need to adopt a new teleological vision or perform some new deontological command; instead, a responsible self might justifiably feel compelled to oppose the oppression of a neighbor. Yet this type of intervention did not readily appeal to Niebuhr.

This last point may be most clearly illustrated in Niebuhr's early article "The Grace of Doing Nothing,"[48] in which he wrote: "The inactivity of radical Christianity is not the inactivity of those who call evil good; it is the inaction of those who do not judge their neighbors because they cannot fool themselves into a sense of superior righteousness. It is . . . a patience that is full of hope, and is based upon faith."[49] The occasion of Niebuhr's writing was the Japanese invasion of Manchuria. At the time, his position was opposed by Reinhold Niebuhr, his elder brother. It could be argued that the failure to intervene emboldened Japanese militarists, who subsequently invaded Korea and the Philippines and eventually bombed Pearl Harbor, thereby forcing the United States into World War II. On the other hand, it could be argued that the decision to refrain from interfering in Manchuria kept America out of a land war in Asia for nearly two decades and thereby saved lives.

It is impossible to say whether or not H. Richard Niebuhr's approach on the issue of Manchuria was morally or politically correct. Although Reinhold's argument appears to be the stronger one, it does so primarily in retrospect. For the Niebuhr brothers of the 1930s, the decision to intervene or to refrain from intervention, based primarily upon consequentialist grounds (which choice would save the most lives, action or inaction), was not at all clear. H. Richard's position was not intended to serve as a model for foreign policy ethics but to remind Christians of the sins that might be committed in what appear to be justifiable interventions. H. Richard Niebuhr held that God is in the process of transforming the world and is doing so without the help of Christians with dubious motivations.[50] He was skeptical of the ethical motivations of many interventionists and believed that the rush to rescue might obscure hidden selfish motives. This position is still popular among ethicists today. For example, John Kelly, an admirer of Niebuhr's stance, writes:

> The theology of doing nothing focuses upon our own sin instead of the corruption we continually see around us. Forgotten in our rush for action is the fact that, as we point a finger at others, they are probably pointing a finger at us. Any response other than a simple act of mercy (the cup of water, the bedside visit, the offer of food, medicine, clothing, shelter) is an attempt to cover our own shortcomings by standing in judgment of others.[51]

In this excerpt Kelly is attempting to interpret Niebuhr faithfully; at the same time he confuses inaction with humanitarian action in the furtherance of pacifism. Nonintervention, however, requires total inaction, so not even acts of mercy would qualify. To be truly noninterventionist would require one to refrain from relieving any kind of suffering through any means of relief. Our debate in late 1992 about sending troops to Somalia to facilitate the delivery of humanitarian aid graphically illustrates this fine distinction. Kelly apparently wants to relieve suffering without changing the political and economic status quo. But in choosing this position, he makes a serious technical error: he mistakes one form of action (humanitarian action) for a qualitatively different response (inaction). It is doubtful that Niebuhr was similarly confused. His commitment to nonintervention was not absolute and, as a form of action, centered upon the inability of the would-be interventionist to have altruistic motives and a disinterested perspective.[52] His moral agent nevertheless is committed to attempting to consider moral conflicts with as much disinterestedness as possible. Yet here is the crux of the difference between homo dialogicus and homo dialogicus marginalis. In contrast to Niebuhr's moral agent, homo dialogicus marginalis knows that there is no such thing as a purely disinterested self that is absolutely altruistic. Since such a creature does not exist, all responses come from fallen, interest-ridden non-altruists.

Given this situation, why should the moral reality act as a constraint on intervention? In other words, the marginalized responsible self knows that she is not a disinterested self, that her actions are not altruistic, and that such is the case whether she intervenes or fails to intervene; that is to say, it is true when she turns the other cheek or when she renders an eye for an eye, and a tooth for a tooth. For her, the decision to intervene is not adversely affected by the absence of altruism: neither, however, can it be justified solely on those grounds. For marginalists of the liberationist stripe, an intervention is undertaken under certain conditions as a response to the prior action of God, humanity, or nature, but it occurs when it is part of God's project for liberation. It is carried out by an imperfect responder to God's prior action. Such intervention does in fact judge oppression and finds it needing opposition and correction. But the liberationist need not be full of hubris in order to oppose oppression. Like Paul, liberationists can oppose the sin of oppression while being aware that followers of Christ are nonetheless fallen creatures and, in other spheres of action, perhaps even oppressors. Niebuhr's desire to avoid hubris is a logical response to oppression from a homo dialogicus. Yet it is unacceptable to the homo dialogicus marginalis to do nothing when something can be done, and to substitute for action the confession of one's sins and the recognition that oppression can be a judgment of God. Niebuhr should have been willing to run the risk of being haughty on behalf of the oppressed. The good Samaritan, for example, may not have had the best motives or have been the one to walk closest with God, yet his action on the road to Jericho is considered superior to the actions of his fellow travelers.[53] Jesus Christ as the perfect responder did not just cry for Jerusalem, while noting its oppression: he also died for Jerusalem. Christ's intervention did not merely consist in a careful examination of his motives for intervening on behalf of humanity. It also entailed taking actions that were premeditated and calculated to transform the world. Nor were his actions justified simply because his motives were pure and his actions nonviolent—that is, calculated to resist evil and to further good.

It is for this reason that Niebuhr's inclination to nonintervention is anathema to James Cone. Cone regards the duty to resist evil, even at the risk of doing so with less than perfect motivations, to be morally preferable to refraining from intervention because one's motives are questionable. One of the most crucial issues to be addressed in our review of responsibilists centers on the same question. At times our marginalists resist oppression; at times they acquiesce to it. From Cone's point of view, all acts of acquiescence may not be morally wrong, but they are all ethically suspect. Niebuhr would freely allow such responses to be fitting in most cases. Clearly, the differences in the two perspectives are immense. Are they of equal value?[54]

Are they both culturally, historically, and ethically relative? Again, these questions will be clarified by examining the actions of our marginalized responsibilists.

Since liberation theology was formally introduced to academic curricula by James Cone, Gustavo Gutiérrez, José Míguez Bonino, Jacquelyn Grant and many others, it has become apparent that although the oppressed and oppressors live in unrelenting tension, they also live in a peculiar kind of covenanted community. It is, of course, a broken covenant, yet its dysfunctionality need not be permanent. If the community were immune to transformation, there would be no need for ethics of any type. However, one of the primary ways of restoring community is for the oppressed to engage in the fitting act of demanding recognition of their humanity and, as we shall see in later chapters, also to fight to meet their own basic human needs. An appropriate response from oppressors would be to hear them and subsequently to recognize their humanity.

A brief examination of one figure who fulfilled his duty reveals that James Cone's militancy has had its antecedents. One of our exemplars, Rev. Francis J. Grimké, demonstrates that marginalized selves can be ethically salient. With regard to the rights of Negroes, Grimké wrote:

> Sometimes, we are told, that it would be better to say less about
> our rights, and more about our duties. No one feels more the impor-
> tance of emphasizing our duties than I do—I think I have done about
> as much of it as anybody—but among the duties that I have always
> emphasized, and still emphasize, is the duty of standing up squarely
> and uncompromisingly for our rights. . . . Duties: Yes. Let us have our
> duties preached to us, . . . but at the same time don't let us forget that
> we have also rights under the Constitution, and to see to it that we
> stand up for them; that we resist to the very last ditch those who
> would rob us of them. And in doing this, let us remember that we are
> called to it by the stern voice of Duty, which is the voice of God; and
> that we need not apologize for our action.[55]

Clearly, in this quotation Grimké is a homo dialogicus marginalis, a responsible self, who understands God's project as being the fight for citizenship rights, and understands that fight as creating duties for all responsible Christians to fulfill. Grimké's response indicates that at least some marginalized people do not interpret acts of oppression in the way that Niebuhr did. Thus our seminal figures demonstrate, by means of their writings and praxis, what it is that the marginalized are constrained to do. In so doing, they qualify the approaches of Niebuhr and liberation theologians.

In fact, one of the reasons that the three figures examined in this book were chosen is that, within a similar time frame, they had to deal with similar ethical problems concerning white supremacy, and they took different positions on how to resist it successfully. The differences in response indicate, however, that a responsibilist approach that is not blindly teleological or deontological may indeed be the best way of addressing moral problems in a variety of circumstances. Indeed, although Bishop Henry M. Turner and Rev. Francis J. Grimké were both marginalized and "liberationist," they had diametrically opposed views on the issue of establishing a homeland for black people. They interpreted the needs of blacks differently, as well as the possible options for response. Thus the way in which each marginalist viewed God, the liberation of oppressed people, and the best praxeological approach to leading a moral life for a despised minority within an oppressive majority constitute the best ethical reflection for leading the Christian moral life. These three figures show, in three different ways, how marginalized people have led morally responsible lives that have honored God, helped oppressors, and yet also aided the oppressed.

CONCLUSION

The ethical potential of marginalized people as moral agents and exemplars is enormous, primarily because marginalized people face all of the problems of the wider human family, and, as Jesus observed, the poor will be with the wealthy always. The mistake that most writers of books on ethical reflection make is that they fail to consider the obvious: the oppressed are probably the group best suited to make moral judgments with regard to the issues of justice and sustainability. The oppressed are constantly beset by assaults upon their individual and group integrity. Because of our physical nonsustainability, we are constantly forced to value and revalue our lives and ways of life. Nevertheless, inside and outside of ghettoes, we sustain ourselves and others with a minimum of opportunities and resources. We continue despite the inability of some of us to develop ourselves fully. To compensate for the frustration of our potential, we have developed the ability to function with grace under pressure.

Each of our responsibilists was able to be a leader in his or her community over a long period of time. Although two were ordained ministers (Turner and Grimké), it is the totality of their leadership and their responsibility to their communities that make them worthy of study. This can be seen more clearly in the case of Ida B. Wells-Barnett, who was a journalist and activist rather than a minister. By demonstrating a prowess in responsible ethical reflection and action, in capacities other than those of the clergy, such exemplars demonstrate that the Christian moral life need not be restricted to ministerial functions or members.

It must also be said that each of our marginalists is an African American and that the primary form of oppression that they fought during their lifetimes was Western white supremacy. However, nothing written about them in this book is inapplicable to other forms of oppression, including classism and sexism. In fact, some of the marginalists featured here also fought against these evils. Still, it should be noted that homo dialogicus marginalis does not have a perfect perspective or judgment. Some marginalists have taken positions of heroism and resistance as victims within a marginalized community; yet at the same time they were perpetrators of oppression within their own or other communities.[56] Unfortunately, the sad reality is that the double consciousness of Du Bois is more real and accurate than even he realized, since some people are both victims and victimizers.[57]

Last, but not least, these figures show us all—whether we are marginalized or not—what might be required of us as good Samaritans and responsible members of a modern, pluralistic world besieged by many problems: outrageous differences between haves and have-nots, deep-seated prejudices, and profound alienation for many people. In short, if the most marginalized people in our society can be morally responsible, we are all obligated to try to discern and to follow similar methods, actions, reflections, and loyalties. The ways in which the most marginalized people act responsibly have not been closely studied. The advantage in learning from the most marginalized has to do with the realization that their actions take place under the most hostile of conditions; therefore, these actions may presumably be replicated elsewhere under equally hostile conditions. The approach of nonmarginalized responsibilists does not lend itself to such ready imitation.

We are all called to assume solidarity with the oppressed: that is, to work with them on projects of demarginalization. In particular, nonmarginalized people may discover how to work with the oppressed in ways that do not overwhelm the latter; thus may the powerful avoid newer, ever more subtle forms of dominance. Most of all, we are called to follow the One beyond the Many, who loves the marginalized in our condition of oppression, and also loves oppressors despite their systems of oppression.

Chapter 2

Bishop Henry McNeal Turner: Responsible Repatriation

Bishop Henry McNeal Turner, as a responsible self in a marginalized community, responded to oppression not as the transformation of unjust relationships between oppressed and oppressors, but attempted to remove the oppressed to a place of opportunity, freedom, and responsibility. Before discussing the actions of Turner, it is necessary to understand his condition of oppression.

THE AGONIZING WORLD OF THE MARGINALISTS

The three responsibilists analyzed in this book were all born in the nineteen century, and they all died early in the twentieth century. To understand them fully, one needs to know what kind of world they inhabited as African-American Christians and whether they were marginalized. Initially, they lived in a world of slavery. The noted economist Manning Marable writes about this world:

> During the entire slave period in the U. S. a brutal kind of equality was thrust upon both sexes. This process was dictated by the conditions of slave production within the overall process for capital accumulation in the south. Black women working in the fields on rice, sugar and cotton plantations were expected to labor at least twelve hours a day without complaint, breaking their backs just like their sons, husbands and fathers. Angela Davis has recognized that "The

slave system could not confer upon the Black man the appearance of a privileged position vis-à-vis the Black woman." Since slavery itself was authoritarianism in the extreme, with the white slave owner exercising physical violence to maintain political hegemony, no "family provider" or Black patriarch could be allowed. "The attainment of slavery's intrinsic goals was contingent upon the fullest and most brutal utilization of the productive capacities of every man, woman and child."[1]

Although the personal biography of each marginalist does not evidence the same level of brutality and suffering, this is nevertheless the agonizing world into which they were born. In this world black people were a despised race; they were alienated from Africa, their tribal identities, religions, and their native tongues. As the property of others, they were unable to interact freely and openly within their own institutions, even in the area of religion.[2] Since their low status was associated with their skin color, they were naturally stigmatized without regard to their actual legal status (Bishop Turner, for example, was born free). Unable to reestablish African extended families or, in most cases, to establish European-style nuclear families, slaves lived a tenuous existence. At any moment, one member of a family, or all of them, could be alienated forever from all previous ties at the auction block.

Although slaves were basically powerless, free blacks were also forced to step lightly during slavery because they were often resented in the South. In some states, laws required them to emigrate or to forfeit their liberated status. Nor did the assurance most whites felt that blacks were inferior automatically end with the end of the Civil War and the abolition of slavery. Reconstruction opened doors of opportunity all too briefly. How marginalized were African Americans after the abolition of slavery? The answer to this question is complex because of the ambiguities surrounding freedom during this period and because of the legacy of slavery. During Reconstruction, African Americans began to re-create themselves. Most were uneducated because it had been illegal, during slavery, to teach slaves how to read and write. Few owned land, because few had been able to buy their freedom or land. After a brief burst of relative independence and near equality, white supremacy swiftly ended Reconstruction and relegated most blacks to positions of subservience.[3] Most ex-slaves moved unwillingly from slavery to another form of exploitation, sharecropping.[4] A fortunate few were well situated because of the skills and education they had acquired prior to the end of slavery to avoid sharecropping. These few were able to fend for themselves, provided they did not offend the nervous majority. Lynching—the evil that Wells-Barnett fought against—was always a way of settling conflicts without reference to any notions of justice. Thus, during this period, whether they were sharecroppers or freeholders, all African Americans were marginalized people, subject to the violent and avaricious whims of the majority population. More important, as Marable notes, the threat of lynching forced blacks to be extremely cautious about advocating sudden change:

> Historically, and in actual practice, it [lynching] is the ultimate use of coercion against Blacks to insure white supremacy. The form it assumes—hanging by the neck, shooting, castration, burning at the stake, or other spontaneous and random forms of violence—is secondary to the actual terror it evokes among the Black masses, and the perverse satisfaction that it derives for white racists. Lynching is neither irrational nor illegal, in the sense that the white power elites tolerate and encourage its continued existence. Lynching in a racist society becomes a legitimate means to check the activities of the entire Black population in economics, culture and politics.[5]

In such a world, one's existence is tenuous and one's identity is subject to challenge at a moment's notice. Yet this is the world that our marginalists inhabited and within which they attempted to do the fitting thing as the occasion demanded.

A RACE PATRIOT

Born on February 1, 1834, in Newberry Court House, South Carolina, of free parents, Turner was more fortunate than most African Americans of his generation.[6] He claimed to be of royal African stock and came from a stable family household, headed by his young mother, Sarah Turner, and his maternal grandmother, Hannah Greer. Unfortunately, Turner's father, Hardy Turner, died in Henry's childhood years. It was Turner's maternal grandmother who was the custodian of Turner's ancestral narratives and who both informed him of his African ancestry and instilled in him a sense of pride in his origins. She also instilled in him a lifelong obsession with learning and self-improvement. The system of slavery, in force at his birth, made it difficult for many free blacks to compete economically. Thus, without much formal education, Turner was forced into a variety of early apprenticeships as a blacksmith, carriage maker, and even as an agricultural worker.[7] Education for blacks was illegal at that time, but Turner was very bright, and this quality was noticed by a white playmate and an educated black neighbor. Surreptitiously, they taught him the alphabet and the rudiments of reading. Soon, by dint of hard work, Turner had read his Bible five times.

Since his apprenticeships held little appeal for him, he was assigned janitorial work at a law office. Despite the illegality of their actions, sympathetic lawyers noted Turner's intellectual gifts and smuggled books to him and even instructed him. Over time, he became literate and was soon converted to Christianity by the revival efforts of plantation missionaries of the Methodist Episcopal church. Turner's own conversion experience was electric—a dynamic response to powerful preaching. In recalling this experience to the white missionary preacher, Samuel Leard, who had effectively preached an especially arresting sermon, Turner once wrote: "You . . . so stunned me by your powerful preaching that I fell upon the ground, rolled in the dirt, foamed at the mouth and agonized under conviction until Christ relieved me by his atoning blood."[8] Such displays of emotion and piety were not unusual for Turner's era.

In 1848 Turner joined the Methodist church in Abbeville. By 1853 he was a licensed exhorter and preached revivals with great success in several states to slaves and free blacks. Nevertheless, despite his obvious ability and call, full ordination was not extended to him because of his race. He married Eliza Ann Peacher of Columbia, South Carolina, on August 31, 1856, while still serving as an itinerant minister; she was the first of four wives in his long and active life. Miss Peacher, a member of a wealthy and devout African-American shipbuilding family, was supportive of his ministry.

An important change came when Turner visited New Orleans and met William R. Revels, an African Methodist Episcopal minister. Revels convinced him to switch denominations. Turner had been unaware of the new, black-controlled denomination, which suited him much better than his own church, which was always ambivalent about evangelizing blacks. Under Bishop Daniel A. Payne, Turner soon became a very successful A.M.E. minister; he served in that capacity for fifty-seven years. He was, without a doubt, an extremely effective missionary and pastor, and the A.M.E. church grew at a phenomenal pace during his years of service. With the establishment of church order came the establishment of independent black institutions.[9] It is out of the creation of these institutions that a new, black, nonslave society emerged. Thus Turner is an important moral exemplar, not just because of his success as a clergyman, but because he was a responsibilist who understood the need for Christians to be active in the creation of new institutions and in the transformation of the world.

TURNER'S UNDERSTANDING OF THE DIVINE INITIATIVE

Turner's interpretation of God is similar to Niebuhr's to the extent that he sees God as initiating action, and humanity as responding to such action.

His God is an omnipotent God and ruled "armies in heaven and among the inhabitants of the earth."[10] His belief in an omniscient and omnipotent God generated an obvious theodicy problem. How could such a God, who was also the exemplification of perfect love and righteousness and creator of all, allow white supremacists to oppress and destroy black people? This difficult question perturbed Turner, but he was able, in Niebuhrian fashion, to respond to all action as if it were a response to God's action. Thus he interpreted God's will as providentially allowing, for a period of time, the enslavement and oppression of black people. Why? So that as slaves they might be Christianized and prepared, once liberated, to evangelize Africa on a mass basis.

Thus Turner believed that the abolition of slavery was the intentional will of God: "When the Negro was being captured, and brought to this country and subjected to a state of unrequited servitude, [God] knew the horrors of their past and present condition and foresaw . . . the termination of their slave ordeal."[11] For the evangelization of Africa, Turner noted: "God knew that the slave regime, although exceedingly pyrotechnical at times, was the most rapid transit . . . to Christian civilization for the Negro."[12] Clearly Turner interpreted God as acting in the world and as using, sometimes unwittingly, slave masters and slaves to do God's bidding. This point of view is, in a strange way, closer to that of Niebuhr than it is to Cone's. However, Turner was no idle theological speculator with reference to evangelizing Africa; he himself made two missionary trips to Africa and worked for the repatriation of all African Americans to Africa for the purposes of evangelization and economic and cultural development.[13]

TURNER'S UNDERSTANDING OF THE SELF IN A MARGINALIZED COMMUNITY

Turner never considered himself to be inferior to anyone, although he did, of course, recognize the degraded state that had been imposed upon African Americans. Instead of accepting degradation, he championed the equality of African Americans at every turn. With regard to politics, he rhetorically asked, "If the Negro is a man in keeping with other men, why should he be less concerned about politics than anyone else?" Accordingly, he insisted upon the extension of all the rights and privileges of Americans to black males.[14] Turner's radical egalitarianism becomes crystal clear upon reviewing his famous address, "Speech on the Eligibility of Colored Members to Seats in the Georgia Legislature." As Turner matured, he grew less deferential to whites and less accommodating.[15] After he was elected to the legislature but denied his seat sheerly on account of his race, Turner declared:

> I am here to demand my rights, and to hurl thunderbolts at the
> men who would dare to cross the threshold of my manhood. . . . Am

I a man? If I am such, I claim the rights of a man. Am I not a man, because I happen to be of a darker hue than honorable gentlemen around me? . . . Do you find me a quadruped, or do you find me a man? Do you find three organs in the brain? If you know nothing of this, I do; for I have helped to dissect fifty men, Black and white, and I assert that by the time you take off the mucous pigment—the color of the skin—you cannot, to save your life, distinguish between the Black man and the white.[16]

Turner believed that human equality was of divine origin, located in God's creative act.[17] Because he saw all humans as being equal in the eyes of God, he considered all acts of discrimination based upon race to be unjust. Thus his responsibility, as a marginalized self in a marginalized community, was to fight unceasingly for the full recognition of marginalized people, or, as we will discuss later, to establish for them new opportunities in a new and free location. Accordingly, he refused to support any "accommodation-ists"—namely, blacks of his generation who, like Booker T. Washington, did not press for the full recognition of their humanity and the rights appertaining to it. A person was not fully human, in his opinion, if he/she would settle for anything less than the full recognition of his/her dignity. He often had harsh words for the accommodationists of his era:

If all the riff-raff white men worshippers, aimless, objectless, self-ish, little-souled and would-be-white negroes of this country were to go to Africa, I fear it would take a chiliad of years to get them to un-derstand that a Black man or woman could be somebody without the dictation of a white man. For the truth is, two-thirds of our race have no faith in themselves individually; they do not have any in each other. . . . There isn't much real manhood in the Negro in this coun-try today. There is far more learning and general intelligence, I grant, but far less race patriotism, and wherever race patriotism does not exist among a people, treachery in its worst form does.[18]

Yet, despite these harsh words, he had great respect for black people. Indeed, to a certain extent, he believed that Africans, and the people of Africa in the diaspora, possessed a greater destiny and higher ability than did any other people. His self-regard and his concept of the stature of marginalized African Americans are most clearly revealed in his comments on the image of God. From Reconstruction onward, white theologians had grown in-creasingly bold in maligning the worth of blacks and in characterizing Christianity as a white man's religion. In 1898, in a public statement intended to rebut these racist views, Turner abandoned his assertions that God was indifferent to color:

> We have as much right biblically and otherwise to believe that God is a Negro, as you buckra, or white, people have to believe that God is a fine looking, symmetrical and ornamented white man. For the bulk of you, and all the fool Negroes of the country, believe that God is white-skinned, blue-eyed, straight-haired, projecting-nosed, compressed-lipped and finely-robed white gentleman, sitting upon a throne somewhere in the heavens. Every race of people since time began who have attempted to describe their God by words, or by paintings, or by carvings, or by any other form or figure, have conveyed the idea that the God who made them and shaped their destinies was symbolized in themselves, and why should not the Negro believe that he resembles God as much so as other people? We do not believe that there is any hope for a race of people who do not believe that they look like God.[19]

His criticism of blacks focused precisely on this point: their failure to overcome the propaganda of white supremacy, including the religious imagery of their era, as well as their failure appropriately to regard and esteem themselves as a race and as individuals. His remarks demonstrate that he understood the absolute importance of the right of marginalized people to define themselves, their God, and their values. Among African Americans, this insistence upon the right of self-definition would not again find as clear and as forceful an advocate as Turner until the emergence of Marcus Garvey. It is a struggle that is still being waged.

TURNER'S RESPONSE, INTERPRETATION, AND ACCOUNTABILITY

Turner's approach to religion and ministry was holistic; he believed that Christians should transform the world. His primary concern, first and foremost, was for blacks. Accordingly, he served his people in several capacities: he was an elected state representative, a postmaster, army chaplain, customs inspector, missionary educator, and, of course, a bishop.[20] In all of these activities, he served faithfully. Yet on more than one occasion this intelligent and vigorous man was thoroughly defeated. Although duly elected, he was never allowed to serve as an elected official in Georgia. In his other secular affairs, he invariably met with discrimination and opposition; these results were simply attributable to the world of oppression in which he lived. Yet he rarely blamed God for his failures. He could find a silver lining even in the horrible cloud of slavery: "Slavery has been a dark providence, humanly speaking, but behind it God hides a smiling face, if men will only see their duty and adjust themselves to it."[21]

Most strikingly, he interpreted the oppression of his era as a providential directive from God to leave the land of the oppressor and to answer a call to create a promised land in Africa. This was often misunderstood to mean that he wanted all African Americans to desert America, when instead he was more interested in the voluntary repatriation of the crème de la crème.[22] Turner knew that many would prefer to stay and work in America. However, what he did not seem to understand was the deep attachment that the oppressed often have to the soil in their land of oppression. In truth, as time passed, more and more African Americans looked to anti-emigrationists such as Booker T. Washington and Francis J. Grimké, and less to emigrationists such as Turner. Even earlier emigrationists, such as Alexander Crummell, who had originally converted Turner to the cause, changed their minds in their latter years and urged Turner to do likewise. He never did.[23]

In fact, Turner's stubborn commitment to repatriation of the best of African Americans to Africa raises the issue of accountability. To whom was Turner accountable? Turner's quarrel with Grimké, who staunchly opposed emigration, and his criticism of Booker T. Washington, the most popular black leader of his era, show that Turner was an independent thinker who was not afraid to go against the tide of public opinion within his own community of oppression. Usually defiant of whites, he was also often at odds with blacks. Clearly, he believed that he was obliged to justify his position to blacks and to at least explain it to whites, and yet he felt no obligation to change his position, regardless of its unpopularity. Even the sanctions that his denomination eventually imposed upon him did nothing to dissuade him from his call.[24] He was absolutely sure of his interpretation and denounced the counterarguments of Grimké, Washington, and others as either failures of nerve or vision or as examples of poor judgment.

In defense of Turner, it should be said that he never lived to see any systemic change and improvement in the life of blacks. More important, he never received an adequate answer to his challenge to his critics, and he refused to change his mind until someone could tell him how blacks and whites could live together peacefully, given the history of animosity between the races. Thus he wrote to Grimké: "Rev. Francis J. Grimké, D.D., says . . . 'It is the duty of the South to do the right thing by the negro and he will give strong exemplification of his manhood.' But suppose the South, North, East and West do not do their duty? What then? Without commenting further upon the remarks of Dr. Grimké, for it all amounts to about the same, may I ask what are these great statesmen doing or saying to relieve the aggregate negro of the condition which makes him hunger and thirst for manhood opportunities and to throw off the fetters which [are] a menace to us? What do they do? What do they say? Where do they go? What plans have they presented to our race? What policy or scheme have they suggested?"[25]

Turner's approach to social solidarity is complex and paradoxical. The paradox hinges upon the response of the community of oppression—the white community—to the opportunity to act fittingly. Early in his career, Turner had sought full equality and interaction with whites.[26] However, after having met with ceaseless opposition from them, he eventually concluded that whites and blacks could not coexist as equals in this country. Thus, although he was not a separatist in principle, he interpreted the negative responses of whites to overtures for nonracist community as logically demanding the fitting response of a commitment to self-segregation. Accordingly, he became an early separatist who found white allies for some of his views in the strangest of places; strict segregationist Senator John T. Morgan is the best example.[27] Turner was well aware of the easy trap of permanent second-class citizenship that African-Americans could fall into in this country:

> If the Negro does not intend to emigrate to Africa and build up a nation and establish himself on that line before the world, as I have advocated for years and still advocate, he must take hold of the agencies around him, fall in line with the white man and march to the music of progress. The negro race of the country is told by such men as Frederick Douglass, Bishop Payne . . . to remain where they are. Now let these great lights tell them another thing. Tell them they must have social contact with Whites if they remain here, or go to the wall. Tell them in the lights of history and philosophy that whoever this white race does not consort with, they will crush out; that social equality is as necessary to our existence in this land as air to breathe and water to drink. This is the indisputable teaching for our young men, if we expect to remain in this country, and the sooner we commence the work, the better for our children.[28]

Here we see the crux of Turner's dilemma; his ecclesiastical mentor, Bishop Daniel C. Payne, and the undisputed African-American leader of his era, Frederick Douglass, were both committed to forging a new covenant for blacks in America.[29] Turner never intended to impugn their character; rather he questioned their judgment. From his long experience with whites, both northern and southern, in war and in peace, he knew that the whites of his generation were absolutely opposed to social integration with blacks. Thus his challenge to Payne and Douglass was intended to solve this impasse. In his reading of history, he found whites to be invariably intolerant of social inferiors; as a result, he considered that blacks were, literally speaking, between the devil and the deep blue sea. They could not socialize with whites because of the obdurateness of white supremacy, nor could they willingly accept second-class status. Since Turner had no tolerance for accommodationists of any stripe, he did not regard second-class citizenship as an option. He instinctively understood the connection between social equality and other forms of power and was always critical of blacks who were unable to make this connection. Of one such mistaken minister, he wrote:

> The negro who does not want social equality anywhere and un-
> der any circumstances, must necessarily want degradation. For when he
> is out of social touch he is out of civil touch, political touch, judicial
> touch, religious touch, literary touch, and every other touch that in-
> volves manhood and respectability. For social touch is the pivotal point
> of every form of respectability.[30]

Thus the call to Africa appeared to him to be the only logical conclusion to the ongoing problem. Yet, although he was antagonistic to many of the whites of his era, he still saw them as being in some sort of covenant with blacks, but he maintained that they had failed to live in that inclusive covenant with blacks as one Christian family in America. He felt that they could at least make up for their failure by assisting in the emigration of some blacks to Africa. He wrote: "We gave the white man our labor, yes! . . . In return he should have educated us, taught us to read and write, at least, and seen that Africa was well-supplied with missionaries."[31] He held the United States accountable for the grand project of repatriation; according to his estimate, the government owed blacks $40 billion: $100 a year for two million blacks' work, for two hundred years. Yet he never got much white support for these ideas except from the racist American Colonization Society, which simply wanted to rid America of its black population.

It is not unfair to say that Turner was less than fully accountable to blacks, particularly those who opposed his ideas; in this respect, he had demagogic tendencies. He was too sure of himself. If you opposed him and were a member of the black middle class, you were automatically considered to be an accommodationist traitor. If you were poor and disagreed, you were a lazy lackey. Ironically, on his own missionary journeys, Turner was more respectful and deferential to African natives than he was to the black population in the United States. Of course, these Africans were the same people who, upon occasion, he referred to as heathens. It was also ironic that Turner probably helped to inspire more black nationalist sentiment and revolutionary spirit on a trip to South Africa than he ever did in this country.[32] Yet, although he was never successful in getting substantial numbers of blacks to return to Africa, his criticism of America, white Christianity, and black accommodationism were all fitting responses to the world in which he was born. Indeed, although his vision that the best and brightest of blacks should repatriate to Africa, to create new civilizations of Christian African genius, seems rather odd, it seems so primarily in hindsight, to the *modern* interpreter. With the decolonization of Africa, and the creation of modern African states, the notion of African Americans going over to Africa and founding new states suggests a new and perverse sort of moral, political, and economic imperialism for modern Americans, whether black or white. And so it should, given the benighted record of African-American contributions in Liberia.

What is most disturbing about Turner's plan is his idea that Africans of his generation were culturally inferior to Westerners. Unfortunately, he was never able to make the distinction between qualitatively different concerns—that is, between economics, technological competence, and efficiency and cultural competence. Thus he confused the technological deficiencies in Africa—for instance, the lack of modern infrastructure and industries—with the state of African's culture, which was, of course, in no way primitive or inferior to that of any other culture. As a result, he was not really prepared to go to Africa and work with and under Africans, and he was equally unready to develop the tribal nations that were already in place. He was therefore accountable to Africans only in culturally inappropriate ways that also posed moral problems.

TURNER'S CONVENTIONAL CHRISTOLOGY AND THE PROJECT OF GOD

What is so striking about Turner's approach to ethical living and Christianity is his absolutely radical (for his generation) idea about God. He believed that for blacks, God is black, without logically extending that idea to Jesus. His God is a God with a project, that of Christianizing the world, including Africa, and doing so by means of Christianized African Americans. Yet he has no characterization of Jesus that logically coheres with this radicalness. As far as it can be discerned today, Turner's understanding of Jesus was conventional and in accordance with the black Christianity of his era. Like most blacks, he believed in the motto of the A.M.E. church: "God our father; man our brother, and Christ our Redeemer."[33] So Turner as a responsibilist is an activist and an interventionist, not because of Christ, but because of his activist God. His failure to construct a new Christology may also be due to the fact that he never had an opportunity to employ any modern hermeneutics of suspicion to the texts, although he was aware of the ideological distortion of the Bible that had traditionally been perpetrated by white scholars. In 1895, Turner noted, with reference to *The Womans' Bible*, a new feminist interpretation led by Elizabeth Cady Stanton, that blacks should probably do a similar revision:

> The white man's digest of Christianity or Bible doctrines are not suited to the wants, manhood growth, and progress of the Negro. Indeed he has colored the Bible in his translation to suit the white man, and made it in many respects, objectionable to the Negro. And until a company of learned black men shall rise up and retranslate the Bible, it will not be wholly acceptable and in keeping with the higher conceptions of the black man. . . . We need a new translation of the Bible for colored churches.[34]

Although Turner did not come up with a systematic reinterpretation of the Bible, he did have, as do most modern liberation theologians, a preferential option for the poor and disenfranchised. Turner's preferential option for the weak and poor is most clearly expressed in a letter to his son. After advising his son in the traditional virtues of honesty, charity, and meekness, he wrote: "There are hundreds of people like dogs, if they see a strong dog whipping a weak one, all the other dogs will pitch on the weak. Never let that be an element of your character. Always take sides with the weak, frail and impotent, especially when in the right. God does it. Follow his example, for the strong and rich do not need your help anyway."[35] Turner does not even mention Jesus here, not even when he has an obvious liberationist passage such as Luke 4:18-21. Instead, when it came to Scripture, he was entranced with Psalms 68:31, "Let bronze be brought from Egypt; let Ethiopia hasten to stretch out its hands to God."[36] In short, Turner was thoroughly theocentric and assigned no particular liberating duties to Christ.

Diplomacy was not one of Turner's strong suits. As a leader, he could be blunt and quick to criticize. Yet his understanding of his call to attend to the project of God made him relentless; he believed that he had discerned the will of God, writing, "Any person who opposes the return of a sufficient number of [Africa's] descendants to begin the grand work, which in the near future will be consummated, is fighting the God of the universe face to face."[37] Such faith is inspiring, yet it appears to be precisely the type of mistaken jingoistic faith that Niebuhr opposes in his essay "The Grace of Doing Nothing." Turner's greatest error was not his insistence that some

African Americans should return to Africa to help build up new nations; rather, it was his failure to work cooperatively within his church structure to build the kind of ground swell to make such a call a reality. He left himself wide open to criticism by forcefully insisting upon an exodus, without having secured a passage to the promised land. Edwin Redkey comments on this problem:

> Shortly after Turner's return from Africa in February, 1892, several groups of would-be emigrants to Africa, some 300 Afro-Americans, arrived unexpected in New York hoping to receive transportation to Liberia. Because the American Colonization Society's ship could hold only fifty people, most of the penniless refugees from Arkansas and Oklahoma were stranded in New York. Their difficulty brought considerable publicity and much criticism for both the Society and Turner, neither of whom were directly responsible for the fiasco.[38]

Redkey is correct in stating that Turner was not directly responsible for the stranding of the would-be emigrés; yet his constant advocacy of repatriation committed him, logically speaking, to the task of building the kind of structure and support to realize that call. His subsequent inability to build such a structure called for a more qualified and muted rhetoric. Turner also erred by presenting as an absolute what should have been merely a strategic response to a complex and widespread problem. His notion that God wanted black Americans to be free, Africans to be Christianized, and the weak everywhere to be helped by the powerful remains prophetic to this day. Unfortunately, his absolutization of his specific repatriation program as the will of God was unjustifiable during his era and looks even more suspect in retrospect.

CONCLUSION

Turner was an agent of God—a responsible self in a marginalized community. Several writers believe that he helped various independent movements in colonial Africa. Moreover, in a world in which Booker T. Washington, a different kind of leader, was mistakenly eschewing civil and political rights for economic opportunities, Turner's insistence upon the recognition of the full humanity of black people was no small accomplishment.[39] His attempt to rehabilitate the color symbolism of America, in which he appropriated and relativized conceptions of God's color, paved the way, decades after his death, for several black power advocates.[40] His pan-African call for greater contact between African-Americans and Africans is still a morally responsible position, although such contacts must of course be made with mutual respect between the parties, and presumably for purposes other than those that Turner envisioned originally. Most important, Turner never left his community as he sought to meet all of its basic human needs. He did not always listen to that community, but he was steadfast in his attempts to better the condition of its members. Considering his early, difficult years, and his modest formal education, it must be concluded that Turner was a *homo dialogicus marginalis* who did what he could with the skills that he had.

He was no systematic theologian, for he did not bother to tie up theological loose ends; formal scholarship was not his gift. Instead, he attempted to make the blacks and whites of his era accountable for their actions as part of his own project to eradicate the immorality of a racist Christianity. If Niebuhr's efforts can be understood, at least in part, as an attempt to curb the hubris of the powerful, Turner's effort constitutes the equally important task of attempting to restore the esteem of recently freed slaves while simultaneously curbing the hubris of white supremacists. W. E. B. Du Bois, who found Turner's return-to-Africa scheme "impractical," nevertheless eulogized him:

> As army chaplain, pastor and bishop he was always a man of strength. He lacked, however, the education and stern moral balance of Bishop Payne. In a sense Turner was the last of his clan: mighty men, physically and mentally, men who started at the bottom and hammered their way to the top by sheer brute strength; they were the spiritual progeny of ancient African chieftains and they built the African Church in America.[41]

Even though Turner's contributions greatly outweighed his mistakes, for us his faults are far more instructive. His chief shortcoming was his inability to accept criticism of his vision. In particular, he refused to recognize that most African Americans of his generation simply did not want to leave America. Most of them had not received his vision and were listening to other voices. Although neither Turner nor his contemporary critics could have foreseen the death of Jim Crow and the relative concretization of civil and political rights in modern America, Turner could have and should have recognized the impracticality of his repatriation project after talking about it with others and reflecting on it. Furthermore, he should have considered people's responses to his vision and the programs they generated as an answer to his actions.

Instead, Turner became trapped in his own dream. His mistake lay not in his commitment to transforming the world; rather, it lay in his refusal to continue the painful, ongoing, communicative action with the church and the world—including the marginalized—that is necessary for responsible action. Instead of critically reflecting upon the actions that his message generated, Turner simply played a single tune, over and over, increasing the volume of it all the time. An inability to reconsider his call to repatriation hurt his ministry, so that it was left to Marcus Garvey to reinterpret and redevelop repatriation possibilities. Thus, despite his triumph of the spirit, Turner did not wield as much influence as one might expect. His refusal to listen carefully to others diminished his stature, and this constitutes the tragedy of Henry McNeal Turner, a magnificent responsibilist.

Chapter 3

Ida B. Wells-Barnett:
Womanist Responsibility

Ida B. Wells-Barnett's responsibility is evidenced by her refusal to let her marginalized circumstances force her into playing a passive, accepting role in the oppressive circumstances of her era. Instead, as a womanist,[1] she used everything she had—communication skills, faith, and moral outrage—to stop the widespread practice of lynching African Americans.

EARLY DIFFICULTIES

On July 16, 1862, in Holly Springs, Mississippi, Ida Wells was born into slavery. Independence came to the Wells family only with the end of the Civil War. The eldest child of eight, Ida was given much of the family's responsibility for child care as she grew up. In spite of her faithful care, two of her siblings died during childhood (childhood mortality was not uncommon at that time). Even more tragic was the death of both of her parents in the yellow fever epidemic of 1878. As a consequence, she became the head of the family when she was sixteen years old. Although substantial, these hardships were insufficient to prevent the strong-willed young woman from obtaining an education. Her father, Henry Wells—son of his master and a slave woman named Peggy—had been a skilled carpenter and had encouraged her to get an education. Her mother, Elizabeth Warrenton—an accomplished cook and a deeply religious woman—had also encouraged her learning.

37

As a young girl, Ida Wells-Barnett attended the Methodist Freedmen's Aid Society's Rust College, located in Holly Springs, which had an elementary as well as an advanced program. She eventually obtained sufficient training to qualify as a teacher, and she spent some of her early adult years teaching in Memphis, Tennessee, supporting her siblings and discovering a latent writing ability through participation in a local literary society.[2] Wells-Barnett reached adulthood in the deep South precisely at the same time that Reconstruction was ending.[3] The tenuous protection afforded southern blacks of that era evaporated with the departure of Union soldiers. Similarly, the protection that the 1875 Civil Rights Act provided also disappeared as a result of a series of anti-black federal and local court decisions. It was the reinstitution of segregation in public transportation that had an immediate impact on Wells-Barnett. In 1884, she defied the segregationist conventions of her day by vigorously resisting being displaced from the ladies' coach on a train until she was literally thrown off the train. She sued the railroad, and the lower court found in her favor, but a higher court reversed the judgment and assessed damages against her. This proof of legal injustice and oppression deeply disappointed her. Shortly thereafter, further disillusioned with the limited prospects for blacks in America, she began her journalistic crusade.

The event that most radicalized Wells-Barnett was the lynching of a close friend, Thomas Moss.[4] Indeed, although she was an activist in many areas, she is still best known for her incomparable crusade against lynching: it was this cause that drove her to risk her life, limb, and property on behalf of marginalized African Americans of her generation.

WELLS-BARNETT'S PRAXIS OF RESPONSE

The response of Wells-Barnett to oppression was not primarily based on political or philosophical grounds. Rather, it was an expression of how she understood herself, her people, and the God in whom they believed. After she had lost her lawsuit against the racist railroad, she painfully, yet soberly, exclaimed:

> I have firmly believed all along that the law was on our side and would, when we appealed to it, give us justice. I feel shorn of that belief and utterly discouraged, and just now if it were possible would gather my race in my arms and fly far away with them. O God is there no redress, no peace, no justice in this land for us? Thou hast always fought the battles of the weak and oppressed. Come to my aid at this moment and teach me what to do, for I am sorely, bitterly disappointed. Show us the way, even as thou led the children of Israel out of bondage into the promised land.[5]

In this passage Wells-Barnett reveals her opinion that African Americans should be entitled to equal protection of the law. Thus, despite her status as a marginalized person in a marginalized community, she sought to exercise the rights of a citizen as a fitting response to an act of evil (segregation and violence against blacks), as the occasion demanded. She evidently saw herself as having equal worth as whites (which is why she sat in the ladies' coach to begin with), and, similarly, she saw that other blacks were the moral equal of whites.

Her understanding of God is also revealing. She shows impatience and disappointment in God. And she is unhappy because she understood God to be a champion for the poor and the oppressed, but this God did not intervene on her behalf. The oppressors won—at least temporarily. Still, her disappointment is not complete; she implores God to tell her how to act and what she should do next. Although she does not attribute the act of oppression to God, her plaintive cry, "Come to my aid at this moment and teach me what to do," is an admission that her understanding of the divine initiative, in which God champions the poor, has been shaken. Her cry also indicates that she needs a new interpretation of what God is doing in the world, and instructions as to what she should do next. Having acted as a *homo civitas* in attempting unsuccessfully to claim her rights, she is constrained to ask God for new directions. Her identification of blacks with the children of Israel demonstrates that she believed God acted in the world to free God's chosen people in the past, that God continues to do so in the present, and, more important, that God will do so again in the future.[6]

WELLS-BARNETT'S INTERPRETATION OF ACTION

Initially, Wells-Barnett believed, as did many of her generation, black and white alike, that the claims of molestation and rape leveled against black men as the justification for lynching had some legitimate basis in fact.[7] However, after investigating the lynching of a personal friend and other local crimes involving people with whom she was familiar, she discovered what lynching really was: "An excuse to get rid of Negroes who were acquiring wealth & property and thus keep the race terrorized and 'keep the nigger down.'"[8] Her response to the outrages of the lynch law was immediate and clear. When she became the editor of a local Memphis-based newspaper known as the *Free Speech*, she used the power of her pen to explode the mythology that was being spread to justify violent reprisals. She continued to write for northern newspapers after the paper was shut down. Along the way, she discovered the two main motives for lynching: first, a system of sexual pathology directed at blacks and, second, the even more simple motive of eliminating economic competition.

The lynching of her close friend, Thomas Moss, derived from the second motive: it was an economically motivated crime. His lynching, typical for that era, serves as a root metaphor for the historic marginalization of blacks. Moss and two other black entrepreneurs opened up a Memphis grocery store that was so successful that it offended a local white grocer, who had previously monopolized trade in that region. An altercation was manufactured on the flimsiest of pretexts, and one of the African-American grocery-store owners was implicated. In short order, an attempt to attack and loot the black-owned grocery was thwarted only by duly authorized and armed watchmen from the black community, who, in repelling the attack, shot three white looters. The unlawfulness of the looters' activities was concealed by the white press and the civil authorities, who misrepresented the wounded looters as police officers. Similarly, the grocery was falsely characterized as a gambling joint and the entrepreneurs portrayed as common criminals. Indeed, the owners were arrested on the pretext of having assaulted police officers. Before they could go to trial, they were kidnapped and lynched by a mob that had been admitted to their cells by the conniving authorities. In addition, the major local paper, *The Commercial Appeal*, falsely reported events in so inflammatory a manner that the entire city was in an uproar and a race riot took place in which blacks were randomly attacked at will.[9]

In such a manifestly unjust situation, responsible action appeared to be impossible. However, as editor of the primary black newspaper in that region, Wells-Barnett had to respond as soon as she returned to town (she had been away on business during the actual events), and she did. She learned that Moss's last words before his death had been advice to black residents of Memphis to leave the area for the West, because there was "no justice for them here."[10] Taking her cue from this event, Wells-Barnett began her crusade against lynching in her own local area of Memphis, and she continued it until her advocacy so enraged whites that they looted and destroyed her newspaper.

WELLS-BARNETT'S UNDERSTANDING OF ACCOUNTABILITY

Wells-Barnett was able to win her crusade against lynching because she understood the concept of accountability as it relates to moral actors in relationship to a larger moral world. Quickly discovering that Americans from both the North and South were intransigent in their commitment to white supremacy and hence tolerant, if not supportive, of lynching, she appealed to a wider moral membership—the international moral community, specifically by way of England.[11] Wells-Barnett saw herself as a member of a wider moral community, to which she had certain obligations. One of these was to make white American Christians accountable for their actions. In particular, she was able to call white American Christians to account for lynching and for segregated Church services.[12] She understood, finally, that Americans of her era were too racist and violent to stamp out lynching without the added pressure of international moral censure. Thus her trips to England were an attempt to embarrass Americans and sufficiently shame them in the eyes of the mother country so as to bring about the eradication of lynch law. Much as modern-day South African activists of the African National Congress such as Nelson Mandela have shamed apartheid-dominated South Africa, Wells-Barnett meant to make public and obvious the American obscenity called lynching.

WELLS-BARNETT'S COMMITMENT TO SOCIAL SOLIDARITY WITH THE OPPRESSED

What constituted the final straw for white residents of Memphis and caused them to destroy her press was the editorial Wells-Barnett ran calling into question the sexual mythology of the South that held up white women and their chastity as a premier value. Wells-Barnett's investigations of several lynchings that were ostensibly carried out because of the rape of white women by black men led to the discovery that although sexual relations were often involved, they had been consensual and clandestine until exposure of the relations threatened the reputation of the willing women. Such profound honesty was seen as hubris by the white majority and proved to be intolerable.[13] Yet Wells-Barnett was a perceptive person, and she understood that the lynchings were not only caused by sexual hysteria; they were also based on economic motives. Thus her response was also grounded in an economic analysis. Privately and in her paper she urged blacks to quit the Memphis area for the Oklahoma region.[14] She correctly understood that the whole economic structure of Memphis depended, at least in part, on the labor of oppressed blacks. In fact, when blacks did desert Memphis in great numbers, influential white streetcar managers implored Wells-Barnett to call off her emigration drive, because their businesses were dependent upon continued black presence and labor.[15] She refused their request, and this show of defiance, coupled with the aforementioned incendiary editorial, finally generated rabid death threats that forced her to escape from the area.

Wells-Barnett's call for emigration from Memphis was indicative of her understanding of social solidarity. She was willing to live among whites as long as such a life was just and peaceful. Since this was not to be, she preferred that blacks take risks in a less developed territory, provided they could find the opportunity there to live free and responsible lives. Thus, although she was not eager to dissolve relationships between blacks and whites in Memphis, she was willing to do so if the need to avoid violence demanded it. This stance conflicted somewhat with that of Booker T. Washington, who, although also opposed to lynching, was more accommodationist in his relations with white economic and political power structures. A strong opponent of Jim Crow laws and segregated public accommodations, Wells-Barnett was not a strong advocate for integration and mixed marriages. Yet, although she usually frowned upon relations between black men and white women, she was fully accepting of the white wife of her mentor, Frederick Douglass.[16] She believed that blacks and whites were called to live together in harmony, but not necessarily in full integration. Her trip to New York to write for T. Thomas Fortune's paper, *The New York Age*, represented an attempt to create social solidarity with whites to the extent that it called for the cessation of lynching. It was also an opportunity to be useful in the struggle while the project to harm her was slowly cooling in Memphis. Similarly, she attempted during her subsequent trip and two-year campaign in England to establish social solidarity with other Christians on an international scale. Neither campaign was immediately successful, but she eventually won her battle, although she was never able to reestablish her domicile in Memphis.

WELLS-BARNETT'S CHRISTOLOGY AND GOD'S PROJECT OF LIBERATION

Wells-Barnett was a daughter of the church, but not a minister and certainly not a theologian in the traditional academic sense of the word. Nevertheless, she had great faith in God and a clear understanding of the ministry of Jesus Christ. She was not just a protester and a critic of American racism, but also a Christian reformer. Upon finishing a national tour and campaign against lynching, she settled down in Chicago and married a prominent black lawyer, F. L. Barnett. Soon she was bearing and raising children, and settling down to a conventional family life. While in Chicago, nevertheless, she still found time to correct the segregated practices of the YMCA.

After a few years of respite from her formal activism, she started a new project, establishing a Christian reading room and settlement house in the notorious State Street area, which was known for enticing recent black migrants into night life and crime. Wells-Barnett did not care that she was doing her mission outreach in a disreputable district. Indeed, that was the whole point of the operation; it was designed to be a place of enlightenment for young men so they would avoid saloons and pool halls.[17] It was to be an oasis of enlightenment and self-improvement in a benighted district. Wells-Barnett helped to run the fellowship hall for nearly ten years. She then decided to design an educational institution, associated with the fellowship hall, that would prepare young men for careers in social work. With the help of the Methodist Episcopal Church, she was able to obtain backing for the idea, but only on condition that she step down as the director in favor of a young seminarian. Although Wells-Barnett agreed, the matter was never settled, because the chair of the committee disparaged her for her inability to secure members from the social register of the city to serve as patrons of the enterprise. When confronted with this alleged failure, she replied:

> Well I would like to have had them, I certainly have done all I could to get them interested, but for some cause or other they refused to come in. But then, I said, neither did Jesus Christ have any of the leading people with him in his day when he was trying to establish Christianity. If I remember correctly, his twelve disciples were made up of fishermen, tax collectors, publicans, and sinners. It was the leading people who refused to believe on him and finally crucified him.[18]

Here Wells-Barnett describes a Jesus who is in solidarity with the poor, a leader who calls for disciples among the meek rather than the mighty. Furthermore, Wells-Barnett implicitly condemned the wealthy and powerful of her age, who had forgotten one of the most important missions of the church—that is, its duty to aid the poor. In her mind, this failure was similar to the dereliction of duty by the wealthy in Jesus' era. In addition, Wells-Barnett defended her organization's board of trustees, who were all men with rather low social prestige.[19] Yet she believed that all citizens needed to respond in faith to the needs of the poor and was deeply disappointed when she encountered apathy and resistance among many in the social register set.[20]

Wells-Barnett also believed in a God who intervened on behalf of the poor and the oppressed. This is most clearly seen in her advice to twelve imprisoned blacks who had been falsely accused of a crime in Elaine, Arkansas.[21] Upon visiting them in prison and hearing their plaintive prayers and cries for acceptance into heaven and the promised land, Wells-Barnett replied:

> I have been listening to you for nearly two hours. You have talked and sung and prayed about dying, and forgiving your enemies, and of feeling sure that you are going to be received in the New Jerusalem because your God knows that you are innocent of the offense for which you expect to be electrocuted. But why don't you pray to live and ask to be freed: The God you serve is the God of

Paul and Silas who opened their prison gates, and if you have all
the faith you say you have, you ought to believe that he will open
your prison doors too. Pray to live and believe you are going to get
out. . . . Quit talking about dying; if you believe your God is all powerful, believe He is powerful enough to open these prison doors, and
say so. Dying is the last thing you ought to even think about, much
less talk about. Pray to live and believe you are going to get out.[22]

Wells-Barnett's spiritual advice was sound from a pastoral-care point
of view. She gave the prisoners hope and organized a new trial for them;
given this second chance, they were acquitted.[23] What is also important about
her theological advice is that it reveals a certain understanding of God and
her formal reliance on God. Her God still performed miracles and was still
available to modern-day martyrs and imprisoned apostles. Her advice also
signaled a rejection of the other-worldly fascination that was an acknowledged aspect of the African-American Christianity of that era.[24] She worshiped a God who could act in history to liberate oppressed people. Such
a God demands that believers also attempt to transform the world. A Wells-
Barnett scholar, Emilie Townes, writes: "She was unwilling to accept the
world as interpreted through the eyes of those who would not challenge the
power structure or who chose to acquiesce to the socio-political circumstances of her time."[25] Thus Wells-Barnett was a responsibilist who saw one's
Christian duty to stand in solidarity with the oppressed and to resist oppression
as a fitting act of moral responsibility. This duty was not derived from any
philosophical argument, but rather from her understanding of Christian
ethics. Her disappointment with members of the social register demonstrates
that she understood that the duty to be in solidarity with the poor was
incumbent upon all Christians—not just those who were physically located
in close proximity to the poor. She fully understood God's project of
liberation and its import in nurturing the self-esteem of the marginalized.[26]

ACCOUNTABILITY AS A LEADER: THE WEAK LINK
IN WELLS–BARNETT'S RESPONSIBILISM

Wells-Barnett clearly understood that the oppressed had the responsibility of holding both oppressors and themselves accountable for their
respective actions. Throughout her lifelong crusade for justice, she called
principalities and powers to account for their refusal to recognize the
humanity and equality of blacks. She also criticized many African-Americans
for their failure to fight vigorously for their own rights. Like Bishop Turner,
she was not an accommodationist, but rather a race patriot. She was also a

womanist who advanced the cause of suffrage.[27] Unfortunately, like Turner, she was unable to lead in consultation with her people. Townes documents this point well:

> The danger in being an agent of admonition is that one can fall into believing that he or she is the only one who has the ability to accurately discern God's will for the liberation of the oppressed. This is certainly true of Wells-Barnett. Repeatedly she forged ahead with her own agenda and methods. Oftentimes this was at the expense of relationships with her peers. She alienated herself among Black clubwomen and with Black and White leaders of her day. . . . Wells-Barnett was excellent at addressing unjust structures, but she did not always remember that people are the ones who help create, maintain, and even tear down those structures. In confronting, the prophetic voice must always keep in mind that a root meaning of confrontation is to face together. The emphasis must be on *together*. If one thrives in a power dynamic which places one over and against rather than with, all prophetic voice is lost. For all her ability to discern and analyze, she could not bring herself into community to communicate.[28]

Wells-Barnett's failure to listen more attentively to other, similarly oppressed African Americans limited her effectiveness as a major leader. However, it should be acknowledged that she always had a tenuous relationship with the black church and was therefore at a disadvantage in dealing with the predominant organization of the black community. As a journalist and a woman's club movement leader, she was better able to fulfill her natural role as a leader, as long as the role was not prescribed in masculine terms. The patriarchalism of the black church, combined with its deference to ordained leadership (a status never sought by Wells), resulted in her often being dependent upon a male chorus for authenticity. Although the black ministers usually backed her, their support ebbed and flowed, depending upon the cause and the mood of the dominant social group.[29]

Yet for all her weaknesses, which included her inability to compromise, Wells-Barnett acted as a *homo dialogicus marginalis*: a responsible self in a marginalized community. She attempted to rehabilitate the reputation of blacks while simultaneously advancing their material, political, spiritual, and social interests. She acted for others after having achieved security and some measure of comfort for herself. In so doing, she took enormous risks for herself and her own family. She did so because she had an opportunity to do the fitting thing that she simply could not refuse. Her actions in relation to lynching in Cairo, Illinois, provide a touching example of her sense of duty.

By 1899 Wells-Barnett had been married for some time, had had children, and had developed some sensitivity to the accusation that she monopolized all of the opportunities to respond personally to problems, thereby depriving others of the chance to act as leaders. As a consequence, she felt that there was a tension between the needs of her own family and the needs of the black community. It was for this reason that she was loath to go to Cairo on one of her standard fact-finding missions. Her husband, Ferdinand, insisted that she go, but she resisted his entreaties. Wells-Barnett recounts what happened after she had retired for the night:

> I was awakened by my oldest child, who said, "Mother, Pa says it is time to go." "Go where?" I said. He said, "To take the train to Cairo." I said, "I told your father downstairs that I was not going. I don't see why I should have to go and do the work that others refuse." My boy was only ten years old. He and the other children had been present at the dinner table when their father told the story. He stood by the bedside a little while and then said, "Mother if you don't go nobody else will." I looked at my child standing there by the bed reminding me of my duty, and I thought of that passage of Scripture which tells of the wisdom from the mouths of babes and sucklings. I thought if my child wanted me to go that I ought not to fall by the wayside, and I said, "Tell daddy it is too late to catch the train now, that I'll go in the morning."[30]

This time Wells-Barnett really listened and she realized that her child was right. So she went to Cairo, a town that was oppressed but not very resistant. Cairo's sheriff, a man named Frank Davis, had willingly engaged in the strange dance of collusion and connivance that is required of officers of the law if a successful lynching is to take place. He had taken the victim into custody, removed him to an isolated area, and then allowed lynchers to spirit him away. Even the black community considered the lynching victim, one "Frog James," to be a ne'er-do-well. Thus the local church was not wildly indignant about his lynching. Yet the governor had suspended the sheriff for gross dereliction of his duty to protect prisoners. Despite this fact, the largest church in the area and several leading black citizens had already written the governor of Illinois to ask for Davis's reinstatement. Davis had apparently extended to blacks some of the fruits of Illinois' patronage system so as to ingratiate himself with the community.

Wells-Barnett met with the ministers and citizens in the area and dialogued with them; she helped them to realize their error in condoning the lynching and convinced them finally to rescind their requests for Davis's reinstatement. She helped them realize that their basic human need for security and respect was more important than the occasional pork-barreled perk that acquiescence might obtain, and she followed up this prophetic leadership with a stirring presentation before the governor. With the backing of the community, and in spite of opposition from powerful forces, including the state's attorney general, Wells-Barnett prevailed, and Davis was effectively dismissed.

This recitation of Wells-Barnett's public ministry demonstrates that when she listened to her family and to others, and engaged actively in dialogue with locals about their problems, she was a very effective leader in resisting lynching and in raising the consciousness of oppressed communities. As for the people who were willing to sell their birthright for a mess of pottage, Wells-Barnett arrested their participation in their own degradation and, as *their* champion, successfully resisted oppression. That she was not as active in listening to and working with other groups is a tragic failure in her leadership and moral reasoning.

What the life of Wells-Barnett demonstrates, however, is that the responsible self must rise to the occasion and do the fitting act, even while risking the possibility of being high handed or perhaps just plain wrong. Her resistance to the terrible practice of lynching allowed for the possibility of real community in achieving the discontinuance of the practice. The mistakes that she may have made in this and other endeavors are vastly outweighed by the good that she achieved. If she had understood, as did others, the "grace of doing nothing" and had done nothing, a race war of some sort might conceivably have broken out in the United States. Similarly, if she and other suffragists had not fought for the right to vote, women might have been disenfranchised for several more decades after 1920. Ethical analysis might describe her actions and causes as deontological, in the sense that they were often rights oriented—that is, her crusades were designed to obtain the right to security for blacks, as well as the right to own property. She fought for women's right to vote and to participate in decision making. Yet the best way to understand her work is to see that she did the most fitting thing for a person in her situation. Lynching was intolerable and had to be opposed, because security from mortal peril constituted a basic human need. Similarly, voting rights were crucial for human flourishing and therefore also had to be secured.

At the same time, it is instructive to see how Wells-Barnett differed from her good friend Bishop Henry McNeal Turner. Both she and Turner refused to be treated as anything less than fully human. Both were critical of accommodationists. Both understood that Christians had to serve God in transforming the world, and they had to do so in various callings, not just from a pulpit. Yet Turner was pessimistic about the possibility of transforming American society; his morally responsible response consisted of advocating a transformative foreign emigration. Of course, Wells-Barnett did push for emigration from Memphis, but only to Oklahoma, another domestic location. By doing so, she reaffirmed her commitment to transforming America. Her response demonstrates that she was a more loyal American than Turner had been; she was also more pragmatic, strategy-minded, and realistic.

In Emily Townes's work on Wells-Barnett, the latter serves as an important resource for the development of an African-feminist social ethic. Townes is clearly correct to view her in this way, but Wells-Barnett is also an important figure who can provide the wider Christian community with a picture of what it means to be a morally responsible person in a marginalized society. She struggled and fought without any assurance that her struggles and battles would be victorious. She suffered oppression and tolerated the inaction of co-sufferers, but she never wavered in her struggle for justice.[31]

Finally, it is important to note that Wells-Barnett's attitude to suffering is much closer to James Cone's attitude than it is to that of H. Richard Niebuhr's. Hers is not a crusade intended to prove her moral superiority by means of stoic endurance or suffering. On the contrary, she fought to prevent the suffering of oppressed people in a marginalized community. Her actions also often raised the consciousness of nonmarginalized people and resulted in their joining in that struggle. Her education of the "haves" often occurred when she was building something, like the settlement house, rather than during her protests against lynching. Indeed, much of the support for her Chicago settlement house came from wealthy supporters of the YMCA, who had not realized prior to her campaign that the Y was a segregated institution.[32] In short, Wells-Barnett was a responsibilist worthy of emulation and a womanist who demonstrated that responsible action could be undertaken in a marginalized community. She also serves as a model for emulation for nonmarginalized people—both men and women. After her marriage to the attorney Ferdinand Barnett, she could have discontinued her struggle and settled into a conservative domestic life. That she did not do so should provoke discussion and self-examination by all nonmarginalized Christians as to what constitutes responsible social action for the haves in a world of many have-nots. Faithful and steadfast, Wells-Barnett gives us a vital glimpse of what the Christian moral life entails in the modern world.

Chapter 4

Francis J. Grimké: Responsibilist as Puritan Critic

A responsible self who responded to the action of God in all of the actions upon him, Rev. Francis J. Grimké did so, however, without ascribing all direct actions upon him as the providence of God. Accordingly his response often consisted of defiant criticism of specific agencies of oppression, such as his government, his community, and his church.

THE GRIMKÉS: A FAMILY DIVIDED

In his own person, Francis J. Grimké typifies the peculiar familial, sexual, and proprietary interests of the antebellum South. On November 4, 1850, he was born in Charleston, South Carolina, the son of Henry Grimké, one of the most prominent white men in the South. His mother was Nancy Weston Grimké, one of the family's slaves. This parentage accounts for his fair complexion, as well as for his troubled childhood.[1] His father died when Grimké was five years old and left him a free ward—along with his older brother, Archibald, and baby brother, John—under the guardianship of Grimké's half-brother (of unmixed blood), E. Montague Grimké.

Although for five years Grimké's guardian faithfully carried out their father's wishes, he then reversed himself and, like one of the brothers of the biblical Joseph, attempted to enslave Francis. To avoid this fate, young Francis ran off to serve as a valet for a Confederate army officer. Two years later, it was Grimké's ill fortune to return to his native city with his regiment, be spotted by his eldest brother, and, again like Joseph, be imprisoned. Succumbing to ill treatment in prison, Grimké nearly died until his mother rescued him and nursed him back to health. Although this saved his life, it also brought him back under the thumb of his guardian, who promptly sold him to a Confederate army officer, whom he served for the duration of the war.

Despite these hardships, after the war Grimké's early years as a second-class "patrician" served him well. A Mrs. Pillsbury, an abolitionist and the former head at the Morris Street School in Charleston which the Grimké children had previously attended, arranged for him to apprentice as a doctor to a Dr. John Brown of Stoneham, Massachusetts. Grimké, however, could never adjust to being treated as an inferior and because Brown forced him to sleep in the barn, he soon set out on his own. He arranged for his own apprenticeship at the shoe factory of Mr. and Mrs. Lyman Dyke, but shortly thereafter, his old benefactor, Mrs. Pillsbury, once again intervened and arranged for him to go to college at Lincoln University in Pennsylvania. Preferring college to shoemaking, he went to Lincoln and in 1870 graduated as valedictorian.

In 1868 while his older brother Archibald was at Lincoln, they came to the attention of their aunt, Henry Grimké's sister, the famous abolitionist Angelina Grimké Weld. She and her equally famous sister, Sarah, established a supportive familial relationship with the Grimké brothers and paid for their college education. The relationship was lifelong, and Archibald named his daughter Angelina after her great-aunt.

After graduation from Lincoln, Francis Grimké began to study law. He interrupted his studies, however, to serve as the financial agent for the university. Eventually, he transferred to Howard University's School of Law. Unlike his brother Archibald, who became an influential lawyer, Francis dropped the study of law and answered a call to ministry. He matriculated at Princeton Seminary in 1875 and graduated with high evaluations in 1878. Thereafter, he immediately took charge of his first church, the 15th Street Presbyterian Church of Washington, D.C. He was to have only one other church throughout his long ministry: from 1887 to 1889 he pastored in Jacksonville, Florida, at the Laura Street Presbyterian Church, but then returned to Washington.

For many years Grimké also served as a trustee for Howard University, and briefly for the public schools of the District of Columbia. He often lectured during his summers at Hampton and Tuskegee institutes, but he considered his pastorate to be his primary calling. When offered the presidency of Howard University, he declined in favor of continuing in the ministry. His congregation had always had very competent pastors, including the redoubtable Henry Highland Garnet. Thus Grimké had a rich tradition to follow.[2] Unlike Turner and Wells-Barnett, he did not see himself as an agitator outside the confines of the church; most of his criticism and resistance to oppression in his society came to light while he was the pastor of his congregation.

GRIMKÉ'S UNDERSTANDING OF THE SELF

Because Grimké had had several reversals of fortune in his youth, was a product of a master-slave relationship, and grew up in a world in which African Americans were in bondage and in which they remained mired in oppression even after the Civil War, his understanding of the self is a rich resource for seeing how marginalized selves arrive at self-understanding. First, like Turner and Wells-Barnett, Grimké believed in the essential integrity of black people and in the basic equality of all people.[3] Accordingly, he rejected all racist sentiments that asserted or implied black inferiority.[4] Grimké understood that for marginalized people, the issue of self-respect was crucial. His belief in basic equality had a theological basis. He maintained that "God is no respecter of persons: he looks through a man's race, color, position—looks behind his riches or poverty, to his character, and estimates him accordingly. And this is the principle by which all should be guided."[5]

Commonly known as the Black Puritan, Grimké was also a genuine ascetic who kept rigid standards for his own conduct as well as for the conduct of others. Maintaining the highest level of the traditional Western notions of virtue was absolutely essential for Grimké. He assiduously practiced and preached honesty, prudence, chastity, temperance, loyalty, and generosity to the poor. These ideals were the appropriate standards by which the moral character of people should be gauged; these were also the criteria by which to measure one's self-esteem. Thus, for Grimké, the worth of people was related to their character, not their possessions or their race.[6] Grimké was a radical egalitarian who saw no differences between races and found examples of morality and immorality in both camps. Grimké also understood the self as being embedded in the matrix of society. As such, selves were not atomistic individuals free to do whatever they desired.

GRIMKÉ'S INTERPRETATION OF THE HISTORICAL
RESPONSE OF WHITE AMERICA

According to Grimké, white America had undergone three stages of moral development. The first stage, a benighted one, consisted of the conquest and settlement of this country, along with the establishment of slavery. The second stage, "principled abolitionism," was the highest stage of moral development. Grimké believed that the highest ideals of the biblical and republican traditions were upheld during this stage. He also believed that the blood spilled during the war had been spilled justifiably, in order to uphold the union and to liberate slaves. Finally, he considered his own era to represent the third stage. To him, as the mature pastor of a black congregation, his era appeared to be in a degenerative stage in which the righteous, noble allies of the second stage had either declined or died and the enemies of Negroes seemed to be waxing in strength and attempting to undo the advances of the second stage. From his perspective, black people were obliged to fight for their very lives as citizens of the United States.[7]

Not surprisingly, Grimké's response was also a response to the divine initiative that he thought had been manifested when the slaves were emancipated in the Civil War. In his opinion, God's will was also manifested by a proper regard for and observance of the Thirteenth and Fourteenth amendments, which guaranteed full citizenship to blacks.

GRIMKÉ'S FAITHFUL RESPONSE TO OPPRESSION

What Grimké believed to be the proper response for the person of character to challenges to his or her individual dignity and to the dignity of his or her ethnic group was briefly described in chapter 1. This proper response consisted of unrelenting resistance to oppression, and this resistance consisted of the fulfillment of certain important duties as well as the steadfast, dignified demand for the recognition of certain crucial civil and political rights. Grimké realized that in a modern, pluralistic, differentiated, rights-recognizing society, marginalized people owed certain duties to themselves, as well as to their oppressors. Among the duties to themselves, the primary ones related to the demand that there be no interference in their efforts to obtain basic human needs.

This duty to claim full humanity was the first pillar supporting Grimké's temple of moral action. Like Booker T. Washington, Grimké believed that the pursuit of self-improvement was an absolute duty for African Americans. Nevertheless, he was also critical of Washington because he believed that Washington was too willing to accommodate white perceptions of black inferiority and was also too willing to forgo certain civil and political rights, such as equal access to housing, so as to obtain material gain.[8] In contrast to Washington, Grimké demanded full equality of opportunity, including open housing and nonsegregated public transportation, at a time in which the gains of Reconstruction along these lines were rapidly being recalled.[9] Like most race leaders of his age, he was swimming upstream against the deep and dangerous rapids of white supremacy. Yet in spite of the country's increasing hostility to blacks, he never relinquished his demand that blacks be treated as fully human and that they comport themselves accordingly. In fact, this duty to be "manly" and "virtuous" and "ambitious" made up the second pillar of Grimké's ideals, alongside the first pillar that required blacks to demand their rights. Blacks of Grimké's generation were called upon to lift themselves up by their bootstraps because no one else would help them.[10] Grimké insisted on this point:

> We are not the equal of the white man; nor does he recognize us as such. Not until we have lifted ourselves to his level in wealth, in intelligence, in social position; and this equality is by him recognized, can we afford to lose sight of the fact that we are colored, or cease to hold together as a class.[11]

For this reason, Grimké insisted that blacks had a special duty: "The duty which lies immediately before the Negro, therefore, is the duty of self-development, the duty of making the most of himself, and of his present opportunities. And in order to do this certain things are necessary, and among them, unity of action, the power of combination, of uniting our forces for the accomplishment of definite ends and objects."[12] This cooperation was based, at least in part, on a certain kind of "race enterprise" that was an intentional drive toward ethnic betterment.[13]

Although Grimké believed in equality among the races—if not as a present reality, then at least as the present ideal—he was also an elitist. Without specifically endorsing W. E. B. Du Bois' theory of the "talented tenth," Grimké was a living proponent of it.[14] Educated blacks with high moral virtue, such as himself, had absolute duty to be leaders of the race.[15] Like most elitists, Grimké feared what he perceived as the inclination to "mediocrity" among hoi polloi: "The danger of the Negro is in being content with a mediocre development, in advancing up to a certain point and then stopping, while the white man moves on."[16] This, however, highlights the paradox of Grimké. Although he himself was an ascetic who confined himself to the indulgence of having a splendid library, and although he was highly critical of crass materialists, he was also very critical of blacks who did not aspire to better themselves, who were, in his opinion, "too easily satisfied."[17] Thus he also observed: "If he [the African American] goes into business, and makes thirty or forty or fifty thousand dollars, he is too apt to imagine he is rich, and to relax his efforts. The white man who is worth fifty thousand dollars still thinks he is poor, and works just as hard as he did when he was worth only five thousand."[18] Grimké made a similar complaint with regard to education, excoriating mediocre college graduates who failed to realize their fullest potential by not aspiring to graduate degrees.

The primary ethical problem in Grimké's thought is thus easily discerned. On the one hand, he criticized a debased people for basing their self-esteem on their material possessions and social status rather than on character development and piety. On the other hand, he criticized them for being less than obsessively devoted to the work ethic (commonly termed Max Weber's Protestant ethic.)[19] What remains unclear is how he expected a debased people to amass a large fortune without concentrating all of their energies on the acquisition of wealth. Similarly, why did he suppose that people who had been assured that character and religious virtue were the primary values would be consumed with the idea of improving themselves materially much beyond the point of sustainability? Although Grimké deserves a great deal of sympathy for the long time he lived within a marginalized community that was beset by a variety of critical problems, he nevertheless had a tendency, as his writings and sermons attest, to sound like a modern-day Polonius, a master of contradictory advice. Yet he held on tightly to his polar views, which he kept in tension, and which demonstrate that he was a product of his age. Trained at Princeton in the classical tradition and familiar with Greek and German philosophy, he also shared the unbounded optimism of Adam Smith in regard to the capacity of modern Western capitalism to provide more than enough for all industrious citizens.[20] Hence he believed that blacks in America would succeed eventually, provided they worked hard, lived virtuously, and trusted in God.

ACCOUNTABILITY IN THE AFRICAN–AMERICAN COMMUNITY

Still, at heart, in spite of his concern for individuals and his interest in opportunities for personal progress, Grimké was basically a communitarian.[21] In his opinion, well-educated and talented blacks had the duty to help the less fortunate in their communities. People of attainment were obliged to succeed not just for their own good or for that of their family, but also for the good of the race. Blacks of limited opportunities were to imitate Horatio Alger and, while exercising Christian virtue, were also to display the kind of confidence in the "invisible hand" that Adam Smith extolled.[22] In short, they were to be good Americans, despite the fact that they were not at all regarded as such by the white majority. Accountability thus entailed a duty to fulfill all of the roles in American society: blacks were to be good citizens, obey the laws, and work for the common good. Late in his life, however, Grimké realized that, particularly in relation to the First World War, blacks performed supererogatory acts for causes that were inimical to their well-being:

> I get mad every time I think of the fact that upwards of 100,000
> colored men have enlisted in the Army of the United States—some

have already gone over to lay down their lives as representatives of the Government on a foreign soil, and yet not one of them could enter a single restaurant, eating place or hotel on Penn. Ave. and get a sandwich or a glass of milk, simply because of the color of his skin. And yet, as a government, we pretend that we are fighting to safeguard democracy in the world, are fighting in the interest of justice, of equal rights for all. It is a lie. What we are really fighting for, and what the Allies are fighting for is to insure white supremacy throughout the world.[23]

ACCOUNTABILITY TO THE WHITE COMMUNITY

With regard to the white community, Grimké found himself and his congregation to be in a constant state of tension within his denomination. Being a pastor of a well-known church in an overwhelmingly white denomination, he was inevitably forced more frequently than most blacks of his generation to be on fairly intimate terms with whites. Thus, ties of denominational polity required him to contribute to denominational life. The unfortunate fact that the Presbyterian church of his generation was unabashedly racist—and content for black Presbyterians to constitute a church within a church, out of sight and out of mind, so as to avoid koinonia with blacks—made relations with them a constant source of irritation for all parties concerned.[24] Grimké did not regard it as fulfilling to be in a quiet and passive role in the presence of whites. At the same time, however, he was unwilling to leave the denomination. Thus he was constrained to be a gadfly in his denomination, forced continuously to call out, as did John the Baptist in the wilderness, warning the whites to repent and to embrace a nonracist understanding of Christianity. If there was repentance, however, it never culminated in real inclusiveness for the black Presbyterians of his generation: with regard to segregation, the white Presbyterians proved to be steadfast and immovable.

Yet Grimké never stopped attempting to make all whites fully aware of the injustices of America. It was his ongoing duty to educate them and develop their conscience.[25] He suffered frequent setbacks. In a letter to the newly elected president, Woodrow Wilson, whose fidelity to Christianity was well known, Grimké wrote: "With a man of your known Christian character at the head of affairs, I am sure that the race with which I am identified will have no just grounds for complaint."[26] He went on also to express confidence in the well-founded reputation Wilson had for being a man of his convictions. However, not even a year later, Grimké was writing a scathing letter to Wilson, protesting his allowing the armed forces to be segregated.[27] Despite these disappointments, Grimké continued to educate and to agitate white Americans throughout his life.

As a realist Grimké knew that true social solidarity with whites would only be a reality in the future, if ever. Thus his understanding of social solidarity encompassed the reality that his America consisted of two societies. Like many professional blacks of his day, Grimké sought to make the case for the racial equality of blacks by moving into an exclusively white neighborhood. Blacks of his era thought that if they could be good homeowners and neighbors in white neighborhoods, they could raise the consciousness of their white neighbors, thus making it easier for blacks with less education, economic power, and social mobility to live in close proximity to whites without objection. Grimké discovered, as have many present-day African Americans, that white flight from blacks is based upon the white revulsion to black skin color rather than upon class interests or a lack of cultural affinities.[28] He concluded that solidarity was to be achieved first within one's own community of marginalization. Thus, in good communitarian fashion, he wrote:

> The second thing that is perfectly clear to my mind, touching our future in this country is that, as a race, we are to sink or swim, live or die, survive or perish together. We can't get away from each other. Never mind what progress I, as an individual, may make, never mind how intelligent or wealthy I may become, the social laws and customs that operate against the Negro as a class, will operate against me. His fate will be my fate. We are all classed together, and are treated alike, whatever our condition,—rich or poor, high or low, educated or uneducated.[29]

Despite the complete absence of integration, egalitarianism, or multiracial social solidarity in the America of his era, Grimké yearned for the day when America would be open to all.

Although Grimké was a well-educated clergyman, he was not a professional theologian. Like our other responsibilists, his Christology must be derived or inferred from a reading of his sermons, letters, and addresses, since he did not write a systematic treatise. Posterity is fortunate in that Grimké was quite prolific in his writings, and most of this material is readily available.

From an examination of these sources, a complex depiction of Christ emerges.

Initially, Grimké's Christ does not appear to be any different from the Christ of the Protestant Christianity of his day. Describing Christ, Grimké writes, "He was the God-man. In him dwelt all the fullness of the God-head bodily; he was the brightness of the Father's glory and the expressed image of his person. He was holy, harmless, undefiled, and separate from sinners."[30] To this fully orthodox picture, Grimké added three particularly important roles that Christ carried out: Christ as the friend of humanity, as a perfect human being worthy of imitation, and as moral teacher par excellence.

With regard to the first role, it is not surprising that living in a marginalized society, Grimké would focus on Christ as humanity's friend. And his depiction of Jesus' friendship illuminates his understanding of Jesus as a teacher:

> Jesus Christ came into the world as the friend of man,—not white men, nor black men, nor yellow men, nor redmen, nor brown men, but of man,—of men of all races, classes, conditions. . . . The friend, above all others, that we need, is Jesus Christ. . . . It is a friendship that is a steadily uplifting force,—a force that always beautifies, always ennobles. Out of it nothing ever comes but good. If we grapple him to our souls with hooks of steel, our course will be like the shining light that groweth brighter unto the perfect day.[31]

Grimké explains how Jesus is the perfect exemplar for human action:

> The only really effective way to confess Jesus Christ is to accept his principles, to live them—to follow his noble example. In proportion as Jesus is revealed in us, and through us are we confessing him in the way that he wants us to confess him, and the only kind of confession of him that ever does any good. It is no use to talk to people about accepting Jesus Christ unless we have accepted him in such a way as to show the value of it, the advantage of it, the importance of it in working out the great problem of right living. Unless we bear in our own character and life the marks of its value as an uplifting and ennobling influence, we had better be silent, we had better never open our lips.[32]

One of the main principles of Jesus' teaching that Grimké wanted lived out is what Peter Paris has called the principle of black Christianity.[33] Grimké's interpretation of Jesus as first and foremost a teacher is illustrated by his emphasis upon the second great commandment Jesus taught: "Thou shalt love thy neighbor as thyself." Using Jesus' teachings, Grimké argues for social solidarity across all racial, cultural, or political lines. However, he regarded Jesus as not merely a teacher of the Word but also as a doer. Accordingly, he emphasized Jesus' relationship with the Samaritan woman as an illustration of the way Jesus rejected the racism of his day in favor of inclusiveness. Even with regard to soteriology, he understood Christ's mission, at least in part, to have been to change humanity's social relationships, and not simply to save individuals from damnation or to reconcile them to God. Thus he writes: "He came to redeem the world; to bring men back to God—to a recognition of him and of the great standard of character and conduct which he had set up for the government of all; he came to break down walls of separation and to make all men brethren."[34] Yet for all of the social responsibility that Grimké's Christology displays, the source for his radical moral responsibility may be seen more easily in his understanding of God.

Grimké's God was a god who never slept. His God was irresistible, with an indefatigable will still in the process of being revealed and established. This God was a god of justice who had a preferential option for the poor: "Because God reigns, there is hope for the oppressed, for the downtrodden, for all upon whose necks the iron heel of oppression rests. There need be no fear as to the ultimate result, as to the final issue. Hence the language of the Psalmist, 'The Lord reigneth.' . . . In that fact he [God] sees ultimately the righting of all wrongs, the breaking of all yokes, and the oppressed going free."[35] Because he had an unshakable faith in a powerful God of liberation, Grimké was confident that the struggle for liberation was not in vain. The responsible self could rely on the assurances of the prophet Isaiah about a god who, "giveth power to the faint; and to them that have no might he increaseth strength." Thus without he himself having had clear success in resisting white supremacy, Grimké could still advise the faithful to be patient, since "they that wait upon the Lord shall renew their strength; they shall mount up with wings as eagles; they shall run, and not be weary; and they shall walk, and not faint."[36]

This faith carried Grimké over a very long ministry, helping him run the good race to the end. With a God concerned with love, righteousness, and justice, and concerned with vertical and horizontal relationships, Grimké was able to struggle year after year, able to comfort marginalized people, and strong enough to challenge them and to oppose oppression.

A RESPONSIBLE SELF? A CRITICAL ASSESSMENT OF GRIMKÉ

A man of great dignity, Grimké could not tolerate self-effacement in himself or others. Like Turner and Wells-Barnett, he knew that black people had to have their basic needs met: jobs, housing, security, and a proper diet. As they had been, so was he a champion fighting for opportunities for black people to meet their basic needs. However, the issue of freedom and integrity was even more important than these basic needs. Having come out of slavery, he knew that blacks could not escape debasement without a strong and positive self-regard. He also knew that to have and to maintain such self-regard, they would have to be able to accomplish certain goals that would serve as evidence, to themselves and others, that they were in fact a people of note and distinction.

In addition, Grimké knew that many of the things that the blacks of his day needed to accomplish would be impossible or difficult if they were barred from the opportunities to do so. Furthermore, in contrast to Booker T. Washington, he knew that conceding social and political equality with whites—even for strategic purposes, so as to obtain immediate economic concessions—was doomed to failure because of the internal contradictions inherent in such an approach. Thus, as a minister of the Gospel, he had to engage in a private and public ministry that involved agitating for the full recognition of blacks as human beings and for their human rights. At the same time, he faithfully exhorted accommodationists and ne'er-do-wells within his community of marginalization to come to a God who could make them free and whole. He insisted that their reconciliation inevitably hinged on a covenant of love and righteousness, in which they were to manifest steadfast loyalty to God, solidarity to each other, and a certain ascetic, unrelenting virtue as evidence of their relationship with God and of their fitness as a race and people. Such a covenant was possible because of the absolute greatness, compassion, and righteousness of his interactive, liberating God.

Grimké manifested his responsibility in the totality of his life—by his pastorate, his private life, his marriage, and his interaction with powerful people and with the oppressed. Like Wells-Barnett, he opposed lynching and supported temperance.[37] Like Turner, he rejected accommodationism root and branch and demanded respect for black people; on this point he finally broke with Booker T. Washington and allied himself with W. E. B. Du Bois. Most important, like our other responsibilists, Grimké was a race leader, a member of a despised community who never left that community or its cause. Unashamed of his partisanship for blacks, he was nevertheless an exemplar of black Christian racial inclusiveness.[38] Opposed to Turner's "back to Africa" sentiments, he nevertheless corresponded frequently and warmly with Edward Blyden, the world's best-known pan-Africanist of that time.[39] All in all, Grimké presents a more complete picture of moral responsibility than does Turner, although some of Turner's failings may be attributable to his more limited educational opportunities.

Yet for all of his faithfulness, piety, courage, and insight, Grimké demonstrated several important flaws in his understanding of moral responsibility. The most important of these is his irrepressible confidence in American capitalism.[40]

Grimké's meteoric rise from slavery and his own innate genius made it difficult for him to understand the limited economic opportunity that was available to most Americans of his era. Most Americans did not have a college education, well-educated aunts to help them, and degrees from outstanding universities (as did Archibald and Francis). Thus the bromides about self-betterment that Grimké delivered to his congregation (which was primarily a middle-class and well-educated group, at a time when most African Americans were not) made great sense to them. Many of them had had similar experiences in overcoming difficult beginnings. Although Grimké's demand for excellence is well founded, and his linking of excellence in performing one's duties to success in business is similarly justified (that is to say, success in business will tend to go to the builder of a better mousetrap), his confidence in capitalism and its ability to meet the needs of people is nonetheless highly questionable. But to criticize Grimké's economic perspicacity, or lack thereof, is not to indict Grimké as much as it is to indict American Christianity and modern capitalism.

Grimké lived at a time in which black people were attempting to go from being unwilling units of economic production (as slaves or share-croppers) to being captains of industry by charting the courses of their own economic souls. In such an age, black mercantilism was understood to be a primary weapon in resisting white supremacy. Booker T. Washington's approach, which emphasized self-help along with the mastery of agrarian and guild skills, proved to be attractive to many blacks, including Grimké. His disagreement with Washington had to do with the latter's self-effacement and the relinquishment of civil and political rights, but not with Washington's basic economic theory. Since Grimké's brother Archibald had graduated from Harvard Law School and had set up a going practice, Francis assumed that all other blacks who were hard-working could have equal success. Grimké grasped fully the truth in American capitalism, that anyone in America could succeed, provided he or she was not held down by the snares of racism. What he did not ask was whether *everyone* could succeed in America. Even in Grimké's era, there were numerous poor whites who had not succeeded, despite having had no limitations set on their life chances. They even had had privileges bestowed on them that had been denied the blacks of their era, and yet they remained poor. This sobering reality might have given pause to a thinker as brilliant as Grimké, except for the fact that when it came to economics, he was well versed in traditional earning, saving, and investing lore, rather than in economic critical analysis.[41] Furthermore, on technical issues of economic theory he relied upon W. E. B. Du Bois.[42]

The Du Bois who was active during Grimké's productive years (1900–1930) was not the same person who became a radical critic of capitalism or the expatriate who lived in Ghana until his death in 1963. Manning Marable writes of Du Bois:

> Although Du Bois considered himself an avowed socialist after 1904, his militancy was compromised with the optimistic spirit of the age. The Black entrepreneurial elite was basically a progressive potentially powerful force in the battle against Jim Crow, in Du Bois' view. He praised the rapid development of the Black business class in Durham, North Carolina, in 1912. . . . It was not until the Great Depression and its aftermath that Du Bois grew pessimistic about the long-term possibility of a "Black Capitalist Solution" to the Negro's plight.[43]

Grimké died in 1937. For several years before his death he had been hard pressed to continue to function as a pastor emeritus.[44] At the time that Du Bois and others were critically reassessing capitalism, Grimké was mourning the loss of his cherished spouse, Charlotte Forten Grimké, and retrospectively interpreting his own ministerial career. He never reassessed his economic views, and although he was a champion of civil, political, and human rights, he never entertained ideas about economic rights. Whether or not the devastation of the Great Depression ever caused any radical change in his thinking is unclear, since he died before it ended. Along with Wells-Barnett and Turner, Grimké died before the basic sustainability of African Americans had been realized in the United States.[45]

Yet he died in hope, not despair. Responsible to the end, he directed that a sizable portion of his estate go toward the furtherance of the Gospel. Much of his work and his institutions survived him, including the NAACP, which grew out the Niagara movement that he and his brother Archibald assisted in founding. Nevertheless, his uncritical acceptance of capitalism constituted his greatest weakness as a responsible self in a marginalized community.

CONCLUSION: THE RESPONSIBLE SELF IN A RIGHTS–RECOGNIZING SOCIETY

Grimké was a vigorous proponent of the development of character for all Americans, but especially for marginalized African Americans. The virtues that he championed were traditional Western virtues, with two exceptions. The first entailed his making a virtue out of the recognition of the black Christian principle, to go along with the other virtues, such as honesty, prudence, and so on. As a son of the black church, Grimké understood rejecting racism in general and white supremacy in particular was at the heart of the Gospel. Accordingly, a responsible self, a follower of Jesus, had to hold to, and to also give evidence of, being "no respecter of persons." For this reason, Grimké regarded most white Christians as borderline heretics. The second exception involved Grimké's vigorous claims for human rights. Although it is common to consider such claims as constituting an aspect of a deontological ethical approach, for Grimké they were a responsible response to challenges to the humanity of black people as well as interactional attempts to escape from a degraded state—namely, slavery and, subsequently, sharecropping.

In Grimké's opinion, marginalized people who refused or declined to claim all of their human rights evidenced a poorly developed character and lacked "manly virtues." The failure to claim all of the rights commonly considered due to the citizen of his era constituted a refusal to claim to be fully human. It gave evidence of a willingness to be regarded by hostile neighbors as a creature of lesser stature and nature: this heteronomous depreciation was intolerable to Grimké and was at the bottom of his rejection of Booker T. Washington. In short, in a rights-recognizing society, such as the one that Grimké inhabited, responsible selves had to claim the rights appertaining to all other citizens. To do less was to act irresponsibly.

Yet simply claiming rights was in and of itself an insufficient appropriate response in the triadic relationship between society and God and the claiming self. This was particularly true of a marginalized responsible self, such as Grimké. What is clear is that at the time Grimké died, he had been leading his congregation and publicly contesting the roles assigned to black people by the oppressive political structure. Although his understanding was flawed by an overconfidence in the ability of capitalism to solve all economic woes, he was nevertheless on the cutting edge of the moral and political discourse of his era, and most certainly a responsible self.

Chapter 5

Responsible Selves in Marginalized Communities: The Variety of Responses

Our three responsible selves acted in a variety of ways, all of which are morally justifiable. But they are not, of course, the only responsible selves of their generation—others who also acted responsibly could have been chosen for this study. The exemplars of this book were chosen, in part, for their articulateness as much as for their actual ethical approaches. Theirs are not the only approaches that could have been taken; they merely represent some of the options. The actions of our exemplars show us what was thought and done, but not all that could have been thought and done.

Probably, for our purposes, the most important aspect of Niebuhr's *The Responsible Self* is its ability to explain and justify a variety of responses. The examination of different responses herein demonstrates that, in addition to differences in personality or temperament that may have accounted for the varied actions taken by our exemplars, there were also other responses to the racism in their society available to them. However, each responsibilist shared a critical response to Booker T. Washington; as will be demonstrated later, this rejection of Washington's approach, far from being accidental, is at the core of each respective position.

Each responsibilist had a somewhat different interpretation of the prior acts of racism each had experienced. Turner, for instance, was most consumed by the relentless religious, social, and political propaganda of white supremacy that denied the worth of black people, as well as their right, even after Reconstruction, to define themselves, their reality, and their destiny. This opposition from whites served to keep blacks from freely exercising their corporate and individual moral agency. Turner considered the withdrawal of blacks from whites into small ethnic enclaves—in order to avoid racism—an inappropriate response to white supremacy. Instead, he attempted to focus his attention on redefining the character, nature, and reputation of black people, by encouraging them to redeem and rehabilitate the motherland, Africa. By being the best possible Christian missionaries to Africa and by raising up new and godly African states, Turner hoped once and for all to dispel in the minds of all domestic and foreign black people the self-destructive notion that they were inferior and incapable of relating in an egalitarian fashion to whites.

More important, he wished to dispel the notion that blacks were incapable of being an independent, self-sufficient people under God. He believed that the success of his program would reveal the truth to the world: God was no respecter of persons, and white supremacy was not a divine initiative, as it had been depicted; instead, it was a heresy opposed to the will of God. Furthermore, the oppression of blacks by whites that he observed and experienced constituted a providentially employed human evil, used by God for the fulfillment of God's Will (to Christianize sub-Saharan Africa). Although used by God, this evil was not to be accepted or tolerated, but rather resisted. Turner was thus consumed by the drive to help blacks realize one basic human need: the need to be self-determinative, to have and to nurture their self-esteem. Ironically, he linked this need to his call to leave the community of oppression. He considered it to be the general duty of African Americans to develop and enhance corporate and individual self-esteem. The duty to repatriate to Africa, and to evangelize it, was the specific duty of the best and brightest among the African Americans of his generation. To respond appropriately, some blacks would have to go back to Africa and rebuild a black world. Turner was never very clear, however, as to what the rest of black America was to do while repatriates were evangelizing.

In contrast to Turner, Ida B. Wells-Barnett believed that for her generation the most important issue was the basic security of black people in America. Accordingly, she was most concerned with ending the reign of mob rule that had given rise to lynching; this took top priority in her agenda of the fulfillment of basic human needs. Her initial response to the subjugation and destruction of African Americans was thus, like Job, to question God about God's failure to make black people secure in America. Much more important, however, than her questioning was the use she made of the power of her pen and her organizational skills to fight lynching relentlessly. In large part, her success may be attributed to her exposure of the facts about the odious practice of lynching. This exposure came well before the era of Martin Luther King, Jr., who also pointed to the morally hypocritical nature of a European-American Christianity that persisted in worshiping, in an idolatrous fashion, the God of white supremacy, and that therefore either condoned or even conspired in lynching. Wells-Barnett was not opposed to Turner's project, but she did not regard it as the most pressing, appropriate, or even practical response.

As to Grimké, he was a responsible self who offered still another basic response to racism, one that might well be the best and most appropriate one. Grimké demanded that blacks benefit from all of the civil and political rights guaranteed to the whites of his era, without any ideological strings attached other than the fulfillment of the civil and political duties that such rights logically entailed. He considered that Africa was primarily for Africans and that African Americans, just like many other immigrants, were primarily for America. Thus, unlike Turner, Grimké did not think it necessary to create an independent African state as a sign of divine approval and a manifestation of human equality. As a cofounder of the NAACP, Grimké had his feet planted firmly on American soil and he claimed full humanity for black people. His call for the recognition that blacks were entitled to a multitude of civil and political rights was designed to secure a variety of basic human needs. It is this meeting of basic human needs, coupled with the recognition of basic human rights, that constitutes the common thread linking the approaches of these responsibilist selves to responsibilist ethics.

MEETING BASIC HUMAN NEEDS: APPROPRIATE RESPONSES TO GOD AND OTHERS

It should be recalled that two main criticisms were leveled at H. Richard Niebuhr's approach to Christian social ethics (see chap. 1). The first dealt with the unusual flexibility of Niebuhr's approach, and therefore its contextualism, lack of prescriptions, casuistry, or easily discernible goals. Often seen as strengths, these qualities can also be regarded as weaknesses because they result in too little attention given to the problem of constructing a viable approach to moral living from a Christian perspective.[1] I have also questioned whether Niebuhr's approach was effective in opposing oppression in an appropriate manner. It is time to ask these questions again. In a world of oppression, how does one act responsibly? What actions are responsible? In particular, how should marginalized people respond to acts of oppression?

Our exemplars have shown us a variety of responses that have one common thread: invariably, responsible selves seek, among other moral acts, to secure the basic needs of the people in their community—for the survival of the community, as well as to secure the social recognition of the members of the community, both individually and corporately. They do so not because they have a well worked-out theory about basic human needs and its relationship to the survival of a people; rather, they do so because as members of an oppressed community, they are inherently committed to fight for the survival of all the members of that community, including themselves. Each exemplar also demanded that the surrounding world acknowledge his or her essential worth. This common thread—a dedication to the securing of the basic needs of one's community, coupled with a refusal to be deferential—constitutes the direction in which responsibilist ethics must go. A careful look at theories concerning meeting basic human needs will demonstrate why this is so.

The marriage of the "meeting basic human needs theory" and responsibilist ethics is a natural, if not an obvious, one.[2] Its naturalness becomes most evident when considering the question: "How can a responsible self be considered responsible if it does not secure its own basic human needs and the needs of other people for which it is accountable?" This rhetorical question highlights the important relationship between meeting one's own basic human needs and the exercise of moral agency; it also makes clear that some needs *are* absolutely necessary to be fulfilled in order to perform certain duties, including giving one's loyalty to the One beyond the Many (the duty that commanded Niebuhr's loyalty). Yet, for clarity's sake, before continuing this discussion, we should present a working definition of basic human needs.

Determining what constitutes basic human needs is not nearly as simple as it first appears. In a free-market society that allows and even encourages the procurement of most goods and services for a price, needs are never absolutely distinguishable from wants or from desires.[3] Indeed, Nancy Fraser, a noted political ethicist, understands that political discourse and reflection on human needs are at the heart of modern disputes:

> In late-capitalist, welfare-state societies, talk about people's needs is an important species of political discourse. We argue, in the United States, for example, about whether the government ought to provide for health and day-care needs, and indeed, about whether such needs exist. And we dispute whether existing social-welfare programs really do meet the needs they purport to satisfy or whether, instead, they misconstrue those needs. We also argue about what exactly various groups of people really do need and about who should have the last

word in such matters. In all these cases, needs-talk functions as a medium for the making and contesting of political claims. It is an idiom in which political conflict is played out and through which inequalities are symbolically elaborated and challenged.[4]

Fraser argues that the concept of basic human needs has no absolute fixed definition; instead, it tends to fix social arrangements and material exchanges. By this she means that current social arrangements and desired rearrangements suggest the content and function of human needs more than abstract definitions. She maintains, therefore, that people generally agree upon the definition of human needs only when it is couched in generalities. As she explains, more precise definitions tend to generate controversy:

> Thus, we can uncontroversially say that homeless people, like everyone else in nontropical climates, need shelter in order to live. And most people will infer that governments, as guarantors of life and liberty, have a responsibility to provide for this need. However, as soon as we descend to a lesser level of generality, needs claims become far more controversial. What more "thickly," do homeless people need in order to be sheltered from the cold? What specific forms of provision are implied once we acknowledge their very general, thin need? Do homeless people need forbearance to sleep undisturbed next to a hot air vent on a street corner? A space in a subway tunnel or a bus terminal? A bed in a temporary shelter? A permanent home? Suppose we say the latter. What kind of permanent housing do homeless people need? Rental units in high-rises in center city areas remote from good schools, discount shopping, and job opportunities? Single-family homes designed for single-earner, two-parent families? And what else do homeless people need in order to have permanent homes? Rent subsidies? Income supports? Jobs? Job training and education? Day care? Finally, what is needed, at the level of housing policy, in order to insure an adequate stock of affordable housing? Tax incentives to encourage private investment in low-income housing? . . . We could continue proliferating such questions indefinitely. And we would, at the same time, be proliferating controversy. That is precisely the point about needs claims. These claims tend to be nested, connected to one another in ramified chains of "in-order-to" relations. Moreover, when these chains are unraveled in the course of political disputes, disagreements usually deepen rather than abate.[5]

Fraser's analysis is applicable to the actions of our responsible selves in their marginalized communities. Their claims for basic human needs, lodged as human rights claims, were offered as appropriate responses to the prior action of the white supremacist majority, who understood the needs of black people to be minimal, or even in conflict with the common good of the majority. The ability of African Americans to define themselves and to be socially recognized as full members of the larger society in which they were situated is, of course, tied to their ability to meet their basic needs. Part of the process of self-definition is the process of defining just what constitutes basic needs in their society. Fraser clarifies the connection between social and political relations and the responsibility of meeting basic human needs; in any given society, those who get to decide what needs should be fulfilled, and what shape the discussions of needs should take, get to determine the level of justice or injustice. To be cut off from the debate is to be cut off from crucial processes: the defining process as to what constitutes needs; the defining process as to the procedures whereby needs might be satisfied; and, finally, the array of decisions that will alter or create the social, political, and economic institutional arrangements for the actual satisfaction of the needs.

In his significant work *Meeting Needs,* the social philosopher David Braybrooke addresses the problem of attempting to define or to negotiate basic human needs.[6] He offers a "List of Matters of Need":

1. The need to have a life-supporting relation to the environment
2. The need for food and water
3. The need to excrete
4. The need for exercise
5. The need for periodic rest, including sleep
6. The need (beyond what is covered under the preceding needs) for whatever is indispensable to preserving the body intact in important respects.

The second part, though it has connections with physical functioning that make it impossible to draw a hard and fast line between the two parts, has to do more with functioning as a social being. The second part includes:

7. The need for companionship
8. The need for education
9. The need for social acceptance and recognition
10. The need for sexual activity
11. The need to be free from harassment, including not being continually frightened
12. The need for recreation.[7]

Braybrooke's list is a fairly long one, but much of his research is devoted to justifying it and to explaining why further additions to it pose serious difficulties. Braybrooke's primary philosophical principle in support of the basic needs on his list is illuminative for the purpose of this discussion: "The normative force of the concept of needs, in its use for evaluating and choosing social policies, finds concentrated expression in a Principle of Precedence. This Principle prescribes that the needs of a certain human population, the Reference Population, as the List, the Standards, and the Criterion define the needs of the members of that population, take priority over their preferences or anybody else's."[8] Braybrooke's inclusion of the consideration of a reference population and the cultural differences that are found in the world allows him to have a principle that is both universal and particularistic. It is universal in the sense that all societies have basic needs, including all of the individual needs expressed within those societies, as well as the needs of their own reference populations. It is particularistic in the sense that those needs are usually expressed culturally, in parochial ways, so that Braybrooke's list of basic needs is suggestive, rather than definitive, as to any particular expression of need.

Thus, for example, as Braybrooke points out, all societies, provide food for their members. Yet the particularities and variety of expressions of these provisions are endless—for example, the Masai require cattle blood for sustenance whereas the Inuits need blubber. In turn, these provisions form a striking contrast with a vegetarian society's requirements, so that the satisfaction of universal needs is indeed obtained in a bewildering variety of particular fashions. That is why Braybrooke offers his list of basic human needs in no defining or limiting way; he is merely suggesting what constitute the most necessary goods, services, or opportunities for responsible moral agents to secure or procure. An even more important aspect of Braybrooke's work is his principle of precedence, according to which basic needs are always considered as lexically prior to preferences. This principle can be used as a major evaluative tool in the political discourse about needs that Fraser insists modern societies should conduct.

If we ask ourselves why meeting basic needs is so important, we will see that, among other things, it permits the establishment of the necessary conditions for the exercise of any moral agency, as well as the foundation for forming the capacity for acting as a moral agent. For example, severely malnourished people who are trapped in a nonsustainable environment (as in the case of the Somalis in 1992) are also threatened with systemic violence and must find it difficult to act, in any consistent way, as responsible moral agents. Their nonsustainability encourages them to lapse into passivity or to engage in violence, or it compels them to flee their homeland and expose themselves to the expedient, dubious chances afforded refugees. Thus, even a casual perusal of Braybrooke's schema shows why Turner wanted at least some blacks to emigrate to Africa for security purposes. More important, however, were the efforts of Turner and his followers to secure acceptance and recognition, if from no one else other than themselves, in recognition of their success in building new African civilizations.

Wells-Barnett was similarly constrained to fight for physical security, and Grimké was likewise preoccupied with securing a variety of basic human needs.

THE RESISTANCE TO MARGINALIZATION BY THE OPPRESSED BY MEANS OF SECURING BASIC HUMAN NEEDS

Our exemplars demonstrate that homo dialogicus marginalis is inherently aware of the immanence of basic terrors and threats to oppressed people. This is the case because we, the oppressed, inhabit the nether world between sustainability and chaos. Our exemplars, for example, lived at a time in which blacks could not vote, were uniformly considered to be inferior, were not entitled to justice, and, in their youth, were either the actual property of their fellow citizens or were closely identified with a class of people who were owned by whites. Marginalized people in the present share a similar consciousness (see the brief discussion of this in chap. 1).

For marginalized people of both types (infantilized and sustained), securing basic needs is, with few exceptions, always a logical response to the prior actions of God and of others. In modern America—a post-Enlightenment society that is a rights-recognizing society—citizens primarily meet their basic needs in two ways. The first is by means of their own efforts via remunerative work that allows them to purchase food, clothing, shelter, and medical care on the open market. Other needs are met by consensual interaction with significant others in the community and in society. This interaction secures social recognition, acceptance, education, recreation, companionship, sexual relations, physical security (including that of one's family), and some notion of "tolerable justice," to borrow a phrase from Reinhold Niebuhr.

Some of these needs are met by means of the state, especially when labor conditions are such that real work is unavailable. The state is also instrumental in maintaining security and the kinds of political rights, such as the right to a fair trial or to emigration, that can only be handled by a governing body. If oppressors in society threaten the oppressed, sometimes the state will act to secure their persons (the oppressed), as in very recent times when the state has punished a terrorist group, such as the Ku Klux Klan. Too often, however, marginalized people are marginalized by the state itself, as when black motorists are stopped without probable cause and harassed by the police, or when they are brutalized, as in the infamous Rodney King incident. In such a society, responsible selves exercise moral agency, at least in part, by resisting oppression through claiming fundamental needs, in this case fundamental rights, which are often called human rights. Each of our marginalists claimed certain rights, and their claiming, along with other morally responsible actions, constituted fitting responses to the prior acts of marginalization they had experienced or observed in their communities.

So far we have demonstrated, at least provisionally, that the struggle to meet basic human needs, and the ethical reflection that struggle generates, constitutes a necessary though not an exclusive approach in responsibilist ethics, and we have associated the meeting of basic human needs with the claiming of fundamental human rights designed to secure those needs, as well as the recognition of human dignity. If this study has not demonstrated that responsibilist ethics can or should be reduced to a simple procedure of claiming certain carefully prescribed rights or even securing basic needs for all, it is because it did not mean to do so. Fraser's analysis shows that such a process could, at best, only be effective in a provisional manner. To offer a timeless "revealed" list of basic human needs would be reductionistic and would move a responsibilist approach away from any method that Niebuhr might have endorsed into a deontological mode.[9] However, while meeting basic human needs is not itself *the* fulfillment of moral action and reflection, it is a sine qua non in that process. Furthermore, this approach, which was utilized by our marginalists, is probably the best approach for giving better definition and form to modern, post-Niebuhr responsibilist ethics, and for explaining what is probably the best connection between the empowered self and the marginalized self—basic human needs.

How is this so? Consider the fact that although empowered selves and marginalized selves may have significantly different perspectives on God and moral living, they have the same human nature and are equally reliant on meeting their basic human needs. Thus the meeting of basic human needs is a natural common concern of all people, without regard to their different understandings of life; this is true even though societies may not agree on every putative basic human need as it has been determined by another society. Some of the philosophical and theological explanations for this situation follow.

THE NECESSITY OF CLAIMING BASIC RIGHTS FOR MORAL AGENCY

Braybrooke's approach is one philosophical argument for meeting basic human needs that has already been briefly mentioned. Another approach that links needs to rights is that of Alan Gewirth, a philosopher at the

University of Chicago. Gewirth explains the connection between meeting basic needs and exercising moral agency by means of his primary philosophical principle, the Principle of Generic Consistency, which has four main precepts:

> First, every agent holds that the purposes for which he acts are good on whatever criterion (not necessarily a moral one) enters into his purposes. Second, every actual or prospective agent logically must therefore hold or accept that freedom and well-being are necessary goods for him because they are the necessary conditions of his acting for any of his purposes; hence, he holds that he must have them. Third, he logically must therefore hold or accept that he has rights to freedom and well-being; for, if he were to deny this, he would have to accept that other persons may remove or interfere with his freedom and well-being, so that he may not have them; but this would contradict his belief that he must have them. Fourth, the sufficient reason on the basis of which each agent must claim these rights is that he is a prospective purposive agent, so that he logically must accept the conclusion that all prospective purposive agents, equally and as such, have rights to freedom and well-being. This conclusion is equivalent to the PGC.[10]

Using this principle, Gewirth demonstrates, at the minimum, the logic behind an individual's motives for attempting to meet his or her basic needs and for resisting attempts from others (presumably oppressors) to prevent him from meeting those needs, even though he casts his argument in the form of rights claiming. Yet he links rights claiming and needs in a persuasive fashion. He demonstrates that a disinclination to meet one's basic needs is irrational, or, at best, a rational albeit passive way to commit suicide. Although Gewirth does not have a nice, neat list of basic human needs that serve as the basis for his claiming basic human rights, his complementing supreme values of freedom and well-being, which he utilizes as the foundation for his principle, logically entail a list similar to that of Braybrooke and suggest a political discourse of claiming similar to that of Fraser.

Gewirth's rights claiming demonstrates one way that responsible selves can exercise their moral agency properly. Neither Gewirth nor Braybrooke maintain, however, that meeting basic human needs must always be done by claiming rights.[11] Indeed, historically speaking, meeting basic human needs must have occurred in societies that did not recognize rights, since the system of rights is a relatively modern approach in comparison to systems of duty bearing or systems based upon the formation of virtue or character in earlier societies. However, in the modern world in which our exemplars lived, and in which we live, a standard procedure of rights claiming and recognizing forms one established approach for settling legal and moral disputes and for fixing and readjusting social arrangements. Accordingly, while this system of rights recognition is in place, responsible selves have at least one clear method for determining who is oppressive and who is oppressed. They can usually discern that oppressors invariably work to prevent innocent people from meeting one or more of their basic human needs.

As Nancy Fraser puts it:

> From this perspective, needs-talk appears as a site of struggle where groups with unequal discursive (and nondiscursive) resources compete to establish as hegemonic their respective interpretations of legitimate social needs. Dominant groups articulate need interpretations intended to exclude, defuse, and/or co-opt counterinterpretations. Subordinate or oppositional groups, on the other hand, articulate need interpretations intended to challenge, displace, and/or modify dominant ones. In both cases, the interpretations are acts and interventions.[12]

Or, in Niebuhr's terms, the parties engage in response, interpretation, accountability, consideration of social solidarity, and then, finally, further response. Since nonmarginalized people can also claim the fulfillment of basic human needs or, at least, immunity from actions designed to frustrate or deny attempts to fulfill basic human needs, and can do so on behalf of themselves and on behalf of the marginalized, they usually have the opportunity to both oppose oppression and to stand in solidarity with the oppressed. And, as will be shown toward the end of this chapter, they thus have as a prima facie duty, the obligation to stand in solidarity with the oppressed. Although other philosophical arguments for the moral justification of meeting basic human needs and for claiming rights to basic human needs could also be made, it is probably more efficacious to address some of the theological arguments for meeting basic human needs and for recognizing basic human rights.

ONE OF THE PROJECTS OF GOD: MEETING BASIC HUMAN NEEDS

This study cannot even begin to set forth, in a systematic way, a complete Christian social ethic that adequately addresses, even on a provisional basis, how meeting basic human needs functions. Instead, it is possible to address critically Niebuhr's approaches to ethics and to suggest corrective measures and avenues of exploration. Chapter 1 detailed Niebuhr's deep skepticism concerning Christians who take up causes and in so doing simply project their interests and egos, as expressed in the causes, but present them as God's cause. Niebuhr's God is not so easily manipulated, and rightly so. Whether or not the duty to help others to meet their basic human needs is subject to this type of criticism—that is, whether or not this approach is merely an ideological construct—must now be addressed. This question is particularly pertinent when poor people ask or demand that people who are not poor help them, or ask the wealthy to agree to form different social arrangements. Would such help merely be self-aggrandizement and bad theology to boot?

Historical examples are instructive. For example, in the case of a peasants' rebellion, Martin Luther, the great reformer, advised both noble and peasant to settle their differences in peace. Both nobles and peasants desired that the church engage in a political discourse that would assist each of them in their claims. Luther entered into this contest as a religious mediator whom both parties were morally and religiously obligated to hear and to honor. His position on this matter is quite complex, however, because of his theories on the Two Kingdoms and on the issue of human sustainability.

Luther maintained that Christians should never be obsessed with possessions and should avoid hoarding luxuries. However, he believed that secular rulers could not be poor, because they needed land, money, and power to fulfill the duties of their office.[13] It was the duty of Christians to help their neighbors at the same time that it was the duty of secular authorities to secure property from theft and revolution. If it should happen that the basic human needs of peasants were not met, a conflict arose in Luther's general approach. As a Christian, the prince had an obligation to help his neighbor survive, and yet he also had an obligation to perform his political duties to keep order. In other words, Luther's approach was always problematic; during times of severe scarcity, it became morally indefensible. Luther enters into this discourse with a bias for nobles and law and order, and he imposes a burden on the peasants to suffer wrong for Christ's sake that officials were not called upon to bear:

> Listen, then, dear Christians, to your Christian law! Your Supreme Lord Christ, whose name you bear, says, in Matthew 6 [5:39-41], "Do not resist one who is evil. If anyone forces you to go one mile, go with him two miles. If anyone strikes you on one cheek, offer him the other too." Do you hear this, O Christian association? How does your program stand in light of this law? You do not want to endure evil or suffering, but rather want to be free and to experience only goodness and justice. However, Christ says that we should not resist evil or injustice but always yield, suffer, and let things be taken from us. If you will not bear this law, then lay aside the name of

Christian and claim another name that accords with your actions, or else Christ himself will tear his name away from you, and that will be too hard for you.[14]

In this passage Luther is engaging in a politics of needs discourse, but in doing so, he is making a perfectly reasonable response—that is, asking the peasants to forbear from making claims on their society, provided their basic human needs have been adequately met under their feudal arrangements. However, if Braybrooke's Principle of Precedence has any merit, it would show us that Luther's position was at best irrational and at worst probably unjust if the basic needs of the peasants were not adequately met because they were deferring to the needs and wants of the nobility. This question is settled by Luther himself when he notes in his missive to the nobility: "In addition, as temporal rulers you do nothing but cheat and rob the people so that you may lead a life of luxury and extravagance. The poor common people cannot bear it any longer."[15]

So, at the same time that Luther was requesting that the peasants forgo securing their basic needs and requesting that they suffer on behalf of the Gospel, he was merely admonishing the nobles to desist from furthering injustice. This position is simply not responsible. Luther's error consists in imposing two unequal moral obligations: one for nobles and one for peasants.[16] Yet both nobles and peasants have basic human needs whose provision should take precedence over the fulfillment of any preferences. Indeed, if enough peasants starve, secular authorities may not have a viable body to govern. Yet Luther does not instruct nobles that they have to suffer for Christ, or for peasants. Thus the preferences of the nobles take precedence over the needs of the peasants, thereby reversing the lexical priority that Braybrooke suggests is normative, as well as according with the demands of justice. Clearly, if Braybrooke's approach has any merit, then it appears that Luther's approach was not an appropriate theology for meeting basic human needs, at least not in our modern sense of the term. From this perspective, it would not be unfair to say that Luther engaged in the politics of needs discourse in an oppressive fashion, even though he was sensitive to the suffering of the peasants. He was affronted by the pushing and shoving that marked interrelations between oppressor and oppressed. Yet, in criticizing the peasants' attempts at creating and expressing their own theology of meeting basic human needs, he helped suppress their struggle:

Furthermore, your declaration that you teach and live according to the gospel is not true. Not one of the articles teaches anything of the gospel. Rather, everything is aimed at obtaining freedom for your person and for your property. To sum it up, everything is concerned with worldly and temporal matters. You want power and wealth so that you will not suffer injustice. The gospel, however, does not become involved in the affairs of this world, but speaks of our life in the world in terms of suffering, injustice, the cross, patience, and contempt for this life and temporal wealth.[17]

Yet although Luther goes on to include numerous biblical passages in his arguments, he evidences a disturbingly strong support for a praxis of suffering, servitude, and martyrdom, which he assigned to the parties on a class basis. To the modern Christian mind, his position appears to be irrational at best, and, at worst, pathologically masochistic. Given the historical context, Luther should not be judged too harshly; perhaps he should even be excused. Still, it is plain that his approach cannot be readapted to a Western, post-Enlightenment, post-Marxist world in which little credence is given to Luther's theories of a two-level human nature. In the modern world, the most wealthy people are capitalists, not nobility. Too often they are too busy either creating or spending wealth to attend to maintaining order. They avoid redistributing real wealth, profiting by the tactics of clever tax attorneys on the one hand and an extensive system of philanthropy on the other. Thus we are still constrained to ask how human needs can be explained theologically in more persuasive ways than those offered by Luther.

One way to approach this task is to inquire into the origins of basic human needs from a theological perspective. The traditional Christian answer to this question has been that our basic needs are part of our natures as we have been created by God.[18] Niebuhr endorsed this doctrine in his approving appraisal of Augustinian theology. He writes in relation to human nature:

> The good nature of man has been corrupted and his culture has become perverse in such fashion that corrupt nature produces perverse culture and perverse culture corrupts nature. The spiritual, psychological, biological, and social depravity of man does not mean that he has become a bad being, for Augustine insists that there "cannot be a nature in which there is no good. Hence not even the nature of the devil himself is evil, in so far as it is nature, but it was made evil by being perverted." The moral sickness of man, which could not exist unless there were some order of health in his nature, is as complex as his nature; but it has a single origin in man's self-contradictory self-assertion. Man is by his created nature made to obey, to worship, to glorify, and depend on the Goodness which made him and made him good; on God, who is his chief good.[19]

Yet if, as Niebuhr and Augustine aver, God is the author of creation and has made a world populated by people who are not inherently and completely self-sufficient, who are in fact created to depend faithfully on God and each other to fulfill their needs, it is most logical to assume that the meeting of basic human needs is normative and good, and that the suppression or disregard of basic human needs is exceptional and bad. Indeed, Niebuhr again turns to Augustine to analyze human sin:

> A second consequence of the root sin is the social sinfulness of mankind. "There is nothing," says Augustine, "so social by nature, so unsocial by its corruption, as this race.'The society of mortals . . . although bound together by a certain fellowship of our common nature, is yet for the most part divided against itself, and the strongest oppress the others, because all follow after their own interests and lusts.'"[20]

Thus, if basic human needs come from God as part of God's creative action, they are, accordingly, an aspect of our human nature and creatureliness. Human preferences may also come out of our human nature and thus may, in some sense, also be from God, but since they are filtered through the lenses of human will, mind, and spirit, they cannot be accorded the same kind of uncritical acceptance of fulfillment that basic needs are postulated to deserve as acts of God, at least not in theologies that understand God to be superior to humanity in judgment, power, righteousness, justice, and love. And even the pursuit of and the satisfaction of basic human needs cannot be ends in themselves, nor can they be attained in any fashion. The struggle for basic human needs cannot utilize any means for its realization, as even Augustine understood; the danger is that the creature might begin to worship the creation and prefer the pursuit of basic goods that sustain human life to the opportunities to worship the Creator, whose grant of competency and freedom permits and encourages human–divine relationships rather than purely human creature-natural world relationships. Nevertheless, in any theology of human needs, the meeting of basic human needs must be accorded a superior status to the meeting of human preferences for the purposes of social policy formation and ethical reflection, although it cannot, in itself, constitute an ultimate telos for the human family. Furthermore, the consideration of preferences should usually be informed by hermeneutics of suspicion, particularly when the preferences of some come into conflict with the demands of others for basic human needs, and especially when this conflict occurs within a specific Reference Population, to borrow Braybrooke's term. Thus all arguments championing basic human needs are irrebuttably, from a conceptual standpoint, superior to arguments favoring human preferences. One might say that in a just and Christian society, basic human needs arguments assume the quality of trumps in the formation of public policy.

Recently, Catholic theological ethicist David Hollenbach offered one useful approach to the task of moving toward a theology of meeting basic human needs. As part of this approach, he presents a theological justification for human rights recognition that originates organically in Catholic social teachings, which he associates with meeting basic human needs. Hollenbach accomplishes this task by analyzing a variety of papal encyclicals.[21]

By implication, Hollenbach's theology of human rights, grounded in Catholic teachings on human nature and human dignity, establishes at least one theological justification for the meeting of basic human needs that differs significantly from Niebuhr's justification.[22] Other Catholic theologians have followed Hollenbach. Another influential ethicist, Warren Holleman, has a similar approach.[23] Still another Catholic scholar, Drew Christiansen, like Braybrooke, emphasizes the importance and priority of the concept of need in relation to moral distributions: "This normative priority means that, all things being equal, claims on behalf of need have greater weight in both private and public deliberations than claims based on competing principles of distributive justice, such as merit and incentive."[24] Lest this sampling of Catholic scholars seem skewed toward uncritical leftists, we need only consider a recent papal encyclical, *Centesimus Annus*, by Pope John Paul II:

> It is a strict duty of justice and truth not to allow fundamental human needs to remain unsatisfied, and not to allow those burdened by such needs to perish. It is also necessary to help these needy people to acquire expertise, to enter the circle of exchange, and to develop their skills in order to make the best use of their capacities and resources. Even prior to the logic of a fair exchange of goods and the forms of justice appropriate to it, there exists something which is due to man because he is man, by reason of his lofty dignity. Inseparable from that required "something" is the possibility to survive and, at the same time, to maintain an active contribution to the common good of humanity.[25]

Space will not permit a full examination of the work of Hollenbach, Holleman, or Christiansen, nor, as previously mentioned, is it the task of the present study to develop a systematic theology of meeting basic human needs. Such a theology must be formulated with a provisional authority if it is to serve as a valuable resource for a responsibilist approach. Yet it is clear, even from this cursory examination, that a case can be made for the development of a theology concerned with meeting basic human needs for the Christian theological ethics tradition. However, our present concern is whether such a case might be implicit in Niebuhr's approach or whether his approach must be jettisoned in favor of a new theology. As a close examination of his work will demonstrate shortly, although Niebuhr never used a "theology of meeting basic human needs approach," the elements for constructing such an approach may be found therein.

First, however, it is necessary to further clarify Niebuhr's ethical approach. As previously mentioned, each responsibilist fought to help his or her people survive a clear danger to their freedom, self-image, security, or well-being. These responses seem defensible after a review of the contexts in which they occurred, and yet they might be construed as constituting what Niebuhr called "ethics of survival."

NIEBUHR'S ETHICS OF SURVIVAL

Niebuhr writes:

Our actual ethics, personal and social, is to a large extent analyzable as defense ethics or as ethics of survival. It is the ethics of self-maintenance against threatening power that is not identifiable with any specific agency we meet but rather with a movement or a law in the interaction of all things, a law of our history. In our ethics of self-defense we act toward the realization of no ideal, unless continuing in existence is an ideal; we obey no law or reason, unless the law that reason itself must constantly defend itself and the body is a rational law. With our ethics of self-defense or survival we come to each particular occasion with the understanding that the world is full of enemies though it contains some friends. Hence we respond to all actions upon us with an evaluatory scheme: beings are either good or evil; they belong to the class of the things that ought to be or those that ought not to be. And ultimately the distinction between them has to be made by reference to the way they support or deny our life, whether this be our physical or spiritual or social existence.[26]

On the surface, Niebuhr's description of our ethics echoes the ethics of response of our marginalists. Certainly all three activists understood that black people in America had enemies, and each fought to resist their hostile actions. And yet what is surprising and insightful about Niebuhr's approach is that he most closely identifies the practitioners of the ethics of survival with powerful groups and individuals, *not* with the marginalized. In reference to the power brokers, he writes:

In the destructive interactions of castes or racial groups in the United States and in South Africa and elsewhere in the world we must take into account that beyond all loyalty to law and beyond all idealism there is operative in the minds of the defensive group a deep fear of coming destruction. The future holds for it no promise, no great opportunities, but only loss and descent, if not into the grave then *ad inferos.*[27]

He adds that such a group is filled with guilt because of a past filled with defensive responses. Niebuhr's initial description of practitioners of an ethics of survival is that of oppressors, rather than of the oppressed. He describes oppressors as those who have the power and opportunity to act self-defensively; they are also the ones who understand that the present is basically sustainable, and they are therefore committed to the maintenance of the status quo. They are the people who feel they have something to lose, and therefore they are also the ones who believe they have something to conserve. Yet oppressors are not politically marginalized. On the contrary, they wish to avoid the encroachments of the oppressed from the margins of society, where they have forced them. Thus they often oppress others so that they might preserve their privileged status. In so doing (as pointed out in chap. 1), they engage in a kind of moral inversion in which the first in power become the last in righteousness. By making themselves politically dominant, they make themselves morally inferior. Yet even a trenchant criticism of oppressors does not itself promote the creation of a theology of basic human needs. And, to be perfectly clear, marginalized people can also be quite defensive, as Niebuhr notes when he writes about death, a problem rich and poor have in common: "It is this rule of death that leads us to develop our defensive measures of *Thou shalt nots* and that isolates us from each other, individual by individual, group by group, each with the motto, 'Self-preservation is the first law of life.' Idealism and respect for the law of reason may protest, but man continues to do what seems to him fitting in such a history of guilt and fear of loss of himself."[28]

However, this passage identifies the most significant differences between marginalists and nonmarginalized selves. Niebuhr writes as if the drive toward self-preservation were a token of human distrust toward the One beyond the Many. For him it represents a drive against others who are not considered "neighbors" within a covenanted community, but instead competitors in a world of scarcity. But what is clearly a product of human society is not the drive toward self-preservation, which derives from a natural instinct and law that presumably arise out of human nature, itself of divine origin, emanating out of the creative powers of God. The sin, if there is one, has to do with the inclination of people to put a hedge around a hedge, that is, the inclination not only to survive, but also to take and to keep, by force if necessary, whatever they require to insure their comfort. It is also a sin to attempt, continuously, to justify such a taking by utilizing an oppressive political discourse of needs that is skewed to fulfilling preferences for the comfortable, or that misrepresents such preferences as basic human needs. Acquisitions made under these circumstances are always morally questionable, particularly when they are at the expense of others who are weaker, and particularly when they are effected in ways that make the very survival of the weak problematic. In this respect, Friedrich Nietzsche was correct in viewing Christian moral teachings as a religion of slaves and weaklings, who are dependent upon the religion to preserve their lives from the machinations of the powerful.[29] This distinction between God's activity in creating a basic instinct for survival and for attaining basic human needs, and the sinful human inclination to aggrandizement is crucial to a proper understanding of ethical reflection and responsible action.

Our marginalists did what they needed to do. They responded appropriately to challenges to their divinely created humanity, including challenges to the fulfillment of the basic needs necessary for their survival. They also rejected the affronts to their dignity that invariably accompany these acts of oppression. They assumed that God had created them and the members of their marginalized community in God's image and that this entailed endowing them with certain basic human needs that they were required to obtain and fulfill.

In this view, acts of oppression are wrong, not because they are committed in order to preserve life, but because they endanger the lives of others in order to secure the preferences of the powerful and the comfortable. Threats to the possibility of meeting the basic human needs of the oppressed cannot be adequately appreciated by oppressors. Like Pharaoh in the biblical narrative, oppressors frequently give orders to make bricks without straw. Yet a simple disinclination to surrender easily to death is not bad on the part of the oppressor or the oppressed, according to the ethics of survival of our marginalists; it is merely human. Nevertheless, Luther's approach to resolving conflicts in meeting basic human needs must be construed as being implicitly inimical to the real nature of human beings, their needs, and at least one of the projects of God, namely the meeting of basic human needs, which has some biblical referents.

BIBLICAL CURRENTS AND BASIC HUMAN NEEDS

No attempt will be made here to use biblical texts to justify an approach to a theology of human needs. Yet even if, as we believe, the major themes in the Bible do not spell out a specific theology of human needs, the

Bible does describe basic human needs in its narratives and in its admonitions, and it does not appear to be hostile to the approach of meeting basic human needs. Indeed, why do we pray (as we have been instructed by Jesus) for our daily bread in the Lord's Prayer, if not but to eat it?[30] What sense does it make for Hebrews to leave Egypt for a land flowing with milk and honey if the drinking of milk and the eating of honey in a free land is of no real consequence? Even manna from heaven is a divine indication that God approves of the physical nature of human beings, whether one interprets the text as a historical event or simply as an important religious metaphor. This reasoning reaches its logical conclusion with the physical incarnation of a person of the Trinity, who is born of a real Palestinian woman, who immediately becomes obligated—as, presumably, all other mothers do—to feed and clothe him. She must meet the basic human needs of the infant Jesus with the cooperation of an earthly husband, with whom she must flee to Egypt when Herod threatens their security.[31] Thus the biblical narrative suggests the suitability of a theology of meeting basic human needs.

Like the Bible itself, our exemplars make only an implicit theological case for the meeting of basic human needs in their actions and their writings. They do not make formal arguments, since as practical theologians and activists, it was not their task to do so, nor did their failure to attend to such duties prevent them from acting as responsible moral agents.

What is clear, however, from the biblical texts is the fact that God acts in this world because this world is important to God. Moreover, God in the person of Jesus acts most revealingly in the world *as* a responsible self, who even in kenotic Christology, never sheds humanity and needs. Thus, in the person of the Son of God, incarnationally situated, we have a Jesus who eats with whores, publicans, and other social undesirables, to such an extent that he is accused of being a drunkard and a glutton.[32] He is also criticized by Pharisees and scribes for healing a man on the Sabbath, because the man needed to be healed right then, at that inconvenient time for religious formalists.[33] Jesus reminds his hypocritical critics, who are willing to pull animals out of pits on the Sabbath, that even animals have basic needs that God desires humanity to attend to, even if in doing so they appear to violate the sanctity of the Sabbath.[34] So also does Jesus justify David's consumption of sacred bread dedicated to cultic worship, which, it is shown, is subject to commandeering under certain circumstances, such as meeting basic human needs.[35] Jesus must even resist the criticisms of his own disciples, who are angered at the "waste" of a "profligate" woman who has purchased and used a costly perfume in preparation for proper interment, one of the earthly Jesus' last basic needs.[36]

In the garden of Gethsemane, we also see a Jesus who does not relinquish life casually, but asks that the cup of sacrifice might pass him by. Even the Christ of the Resurrection, who no longer has any earthly needs, willingly attends to cooking a breakfast of fish for his disciples, to help them to meet their basic needs. This picture of Jesus is neither novel nor hostile to traditional Christian doctrine. For centuries Christians have resisted Christologies that were Docetic, that is, that denied the full human nature of Jesus.[37] The somewhat new aspect in this theology of human needs is the focus, which, rather than being on whether or not Jesus was human, is on what it really means to be human, in a material sense, for Jesus or anyone else. In other words, what do people need?

PUBLIC DISCOURSE ON BASIC HUMAN NEEDS

The theology of meeting basic human needs that has been previously presented in outline form is not at all complete, or adequate, for the task of fully undergirding a responsibilist approach to Christian social ethics. It is not that the task is impossible; rather, the point is, as Fraser has shown, that it is an ongoing process. A theology of human needs must necessarily be a public theology that at some point somehow enters the system of political discourse. It is not so much a reflection on the nature of God as it is both a theological inquiry into anthropology and a communal exploration of human obligation.

Nevertheless, in a world in which forty thousand people starve to death every day, the responsibilist must inquire into the will and the projects of God vis-à-vis humanity. How is God acting in a world in which God creates so many people, many of whom never get or receive the minimum material goods that they would need to permit them to respond freely to their Creator in anything that approaches an adequate manner? In a world in which somewhere a woman is raped every five seconds on the average, how is God's plan for human sexuality expressed? In a world in which the rich few behave like an international resources cartel and do not share the least bit of their wealth with the desperate poor, what is God doing? These questions lead us back to examining Niebuhr's understanding of God's will. We will see that Niebuhr's thinking on this issue reflects a basic error that corresponds to and complements his erroneous thinking about the ethics of survival.

DISTINGUISHING DIVINE WILL FROM HUMAN EVIL

In the first chapter, we saw that Niebuhr could accept God's will as exemplified in both the fall of a sparrow and the tyranny of a ruler. Yet these two forms of evil are not conceptually equivalent. A natural death is not the same as an assassination. Cain's killing of Abel is not equivalent to God's judgment of Moses. Similarly, the basic instinct for survival exhibited in all healthy creatures is not to be confused with the ethics of survival that Niebuhr rightly condemns. In this instance, Niebuhr does not recognize the distinction between human agency and divine agency, and between human action and divine action. We see that Jesus respects the first law of nature in the garden of Gethsemane when he expresses a desire to live and not to die. Jesus has come to live on Earth as a fulfillment of God's providence rather than to efface natural laws. Thus, he does not revoke the law of self-preservation, but rather transcends it by way of the Resurrection. And this transcendence is accomplished not so much by the power of Jesus as by the power of God in response to Jesus' faith, submission, and loyalty.

In this instance, therefore, death is not good, although it is accepted willingly by Jesus as the fitting response. It is a better response than that of disobeying the One beyond the Many, toward whom Jesus displays ultimate loyalty, devotion, and sacrifice. The law of self-preservation is thereby relativized so that far from constituting the last divine word with regard to human nature and human destiny, it is merely a necessary yet only pre-liminary word. In Jesus' most stressful hour, the avenue to sin does not lie in his natural desire to live, but instead in his possible refusal to accept the divine response and notification that the time to die has come. To want to avoid suffering and death did not constitute sin, but the refusal to surrender to death, had Jesus taken that route, would have been sinful. Thus the tyranny of the Roman executioners and the instigation of prosecution by the Pharisees and scribes in the political death of Jesus are not expressions of the will of God in the way that the translation of Elijah to heaven is such an expression. Jesus' healing of the soldier's ear, which was wounded when one of his disciples met the violence of the Romans with violence, does not represent an endorsement of their authority or connote the righteousness of their claims upon him. It is, instead, an act of supererogation—a relinquishment of his right to life and his basic human need for physical security. Jesus surrenders his life to the unjust; he does not simply throw it away.

What is important to note is the fact that natural evil is not the same as human evil. Oppression as we have described it is not a form of natural evil. Invariably, human agency and human action that are artificial and social, rather than natural, are associated with it. Thus war and the incarceration of people in concentration camps do not belong in the same conceptual category as a cyclical famine, although death by starvation may be the result of both evils.[38] This is a distinction that Niebuhr never clearly realized. Similarly, it is not required by Christian ethics that people suffer stoically the depredations of unjust human forces in the same way that they might be encouraged to accept the results of the destructive power of a tornado, earthquake, or typhoon. In short, responsible selves have an obligation to participate in the struggle for the fulfillment of basic human needs, whether the threat to the fulfillment of those needs comes from a natural or a human source, and they need not fear claiming that their struggle harmonizes with providence, even if it cannot be represented, without qualifications, as the specific intention of God.

THE MEETING OF BASIC HUMAN NEEDS: A VIABLE APPROACH TO UNIVERSAL HUMAN MORAL RESPONSIBILITY

Having clarified two major errors with regard to Niebuhr's approach to the issue of survival in a world created good but in which evil is profoundly manifested—the confusion of natural evil with human evil and the confusion of the will of God intended in the meeting of basic human needs as part of God's creation, in contradistinction with God's instrumental use of human evil to, nevertheless, effectuate God's will—we can now turn to another aspect of Niebuhr's approach, his concept of universal moral responsibility. With the help of this concept, it will be possible to absorb the corrections implied in our criticism of Niebuhr, as well as those implied in the superior praxis and reflection of our responsibilists.

For it is in Niebuhr's concept of covenant and the covenanted community that the theology of meeting basic human needs finds a home, particularly as it relates to his concept of universal morality. It is at this point that the relationship between marginalized selves and nonmarginalized selves may be most fully understood.

Niebuhr writes: "The idea or pattern of responsibility, then, may summarily and abstractly be defined as the idea of an agent's action as response to an action upon him in accordance with his interpretation of the latter action and with his expectation of response to his response; and all of this is in a continuing community of agents."[39] It is by the divine initiative that the self is created with basic human needs, and it is his/her customary response to this act of creation to attempt to meet these needs for himself/herself and for others. This is what invariably takes place within distinct societies. Would-be responsible selves attempt to meet their needs while anticipating that their actions will occur and be acknowledged in a community that is similar in concept to the one Braybrooke has called the reference population. These selves try to meet their needs both in anticipation of the response of other selves similarly situated and in response to the major institutions in their society. In any society, what constitutes the basic human needs depends upon the meaning attributed to life in that society.

Niebuhr employed a concept of interpretation called "internal history" that is appropriately applied to this process. He located his quintessential explanation of the process in the life, death, and resurrection of Jesus Christ. The events in Christ's life have a different meaning for members of a living, believing community than they do when they are merely historical references that a Roman historian might compile. For Christians, Jesus is the Son of the living God, by whom they are saved and with whom they may have an ongoing relationship in this world and the next. For the first-century Roman historian, Jesus of Nazareth is an odd Jewish religious revolutionary who starts a new and volatile Jewish sect based upon absurd religious claims and myths of divinity and resurrection.[40] Internal history is applicable not only to explicitly religious subjects, but also comes into play with reference to meeting basic human needs. Indeed, most of Niebuhr's interpretations of internal history are political rather than religious. For the Christian, according to Niebuhr's scheme, all people are created by God, whether or not they individually or corporately believe in the one that Christians posit as their creator. In a broad sense, Christians are created to be in covenant with God and the world, and they are therefore committed to recognizing the humanity of nonbelievers and their value in relation to God, even if the nonbelievers do not understand that they have a relation to God. Furthermore, because nontheists are valuable creatures, their spiritual and physical well being is of no small consequence to believers, even though the non-Christian's internal histories may be atheistic, polytheistic, or henotheistic, and ours, as Christians, cannot be any of these things. The survival of pagans should be of as much consequence to Christians as it is to the pagans themselves, because of their value in relation to God as God's beloved creatures. Their deprivation or oppression cannot be understood to be theirs alone, and their suffering is an affront to the God we worship and serve and therefore must be an affront to us. Nor can their death in massive numbers because of genocide, war, economic injustice, or natural causes be passively tolerated. The reason for this is provided in the twenty-fifth chapter of Matthew, where we have an apocalyptic image of Jesus, who recognizes that the providers of basic human needs are his true followers and refuses to recognize the practitioners of the sins of omission, whom he gives up to perdition because of their inaction.[41] These "false" Christians have erred because of their failure to recognize that others have been relegated to the status of nonmembers in a universal, inclusively covenanted community. Thus the hungry and thirsty are equally created by God, in God's image, and the false Christians are idolatrous in that they have worshiped a false god who, in their opinion, has not created all people, as is evidenced by their praxis.

Niebuhr regarded all people as members of a covenanted community, even though they may not have assented to the covenant of Christians. By regarding all people in this way, he arrives at a confession of universal moral responsibility. From his perspective, the church is in covenant with others, whether we, the church, or they, the world, like it or not. If Niebuhr's understanding of membership is wedded to a basic human needs approach, then the failure of any group to meet their basic needs has to concern Christians. In particular, since the meeting of those needs should be assumed to be an appropriate response to God's initial act of creation, then if God's creatures are prevented from meeting their basic human needs, we should presumably, as servants of God, consider ourselves allies in their struggle and be equally confronted with the duty to respond properly.

This means that nonmarginalized responsibilists cannot always enjoy the grace of doing nothing. Indeed, the opposite is true. At the least, empowered selves are compelled to actively investigate ways they can aid the marginalized. This is especially true of Niebuhr's approach that eschewed the formal use of abstract terms such as *right* and *good* in noncontextual settings. As the following excerpt indicates, Niebuhr always insisted upon relational approaches that were inherently social in nature: "But, in the interaction of being with being, right is not merely a means to the good; it is the goodness of relatedness in action. It is never definable in the abstract but only by reference to the nature and the relations of beings in interaction. The 'ought' in which the sense of right comes to expression is a statement of what is owed to another being. It has significance in such a sentence as 'A man ought to pay his debts to his creditors,' since he is bound to his creditors in an actual community of interdependent life.[42] Thus, employing a Niebuhrian category, we have an obligation to intervene, if necessary, in the struggle of others to survive if they cannot meet their own basic human needs; we must do this because, whether we are marginalized or empowered selves, we are in a relationship of some kind with them.[43] Yet Niebuhr's position on this matter is incomplete without a consideration of external history, the polar opposite of internal history.

External history is characterized, of course, by the dispassionate, disinterestedness of the foreign, nonconfessing community.[44] In the example used above, the basically indifferent attitude of a Roman historian is his expression, from a Christian point of view, of external history: for him, Jesus is just another Jewish cult leader. The reality of the existence of differing views in internal history and external history must be applied to the issue of meeting basic human needs. From the point of view of the marginalized Christian, God has created human beings with basic human needs, and we are all called to seek to fulfill them continuously by the very act of creation. This summons arrives without the need of any additional support by means of a special divine revelation. Yet the appropriateness of helping people to meet their basic needs is known not only by Christians, but also by non-Christians. Believers can look at what all people are doing around the world and come to the same conclusion—that it is, generally speaking, appropriate to help people meet their basic needs. Phenomeno-logically speaking, all people are attempting to define their basic human needs, and we are all attempting to fulfill them. The provincial interpre-tations given the symbolic meanings of the needs does not obscure either the universal attempt or the universal requirement to fulfill them. Philo-sophical systems such as Braybrooke's, Fraser's, and Gewirth's simply ex-plain, as best they can and in rational terms, how and why everyone is attending to these basic tasks. These philosophers attempt to show the appropriateness of the conclusions we have teased out of Niebuhr's phe-nomenological approach, which is centrally featured in his theological ethics. In doing so, they have sought to create a kind of universal moral responsibility grounded in human reason and human biology that is, from a Niebuhrian point of view, simply a natural manifestation of the Divine Self's revelation of creation and the opportunity for finite selves to exist in relation to the Divine Self. Thus the natural revelation in creation testifies to the special revelation of God that Christians have received as the gospel of Jesus Christ. It is this same revelation that is also centrally featured in the internal history given to the biblical authors, and in the living witness of the believing community and in its traditions.

Despite the apparent congruity of a theology of meeting basic human needs with Niebuhr's responsibilist approach, this is not an approach that Niebuhr himself actually recognized and endorsed; it was, however, implicit in his approach. Furthermore, it is this kind of ethical approach that a responsibilist can and should embrace. Niebuhr associated the concept of responsibility with an approach not unlike that of Nancy Fraser—that is, he viewed responsibility as a kind of continuous conversation: "I engage rather in a continuous dialogue in which there are at least these three partners—the self, the social companion, and natural events."[45] Obviously, although Niebuhr never addressed these issues, basic human needs are invariably inherent in relationships with social companions and in regard to natural events such as those that produce hunger, cold, and the like. Thus the meeting of basic human needs *is always a subtext* in any of the dialogues that the self and the social companion could ever have had, whether Niebuhr understood this or not.

Niebuhr also had a second understanding of a basic triadic relationship:

> The responsive self, however, exists in another triadic, dialectical interaction. . . . The second triadic situation in which we find ourselves responding and responsible is the one my countryman Josiah Royce has described with the aid of the idea of the cause. . . . Instead of thinking of man as realizer of ideals or as obedient to laws he saw him as one who comes to selfhood by committing himself to a cause.[46]

Niebuhr joins Royce in this concept and specifically associates the cause with both the individual self and a "transcendent" reference group as carriers of the cause. These transcendent personalities personify responsible selves of prior generations who crystallized the identity of the cause of their society and who subsequently fought to maintain it. They realized themselves more fully in the struggle for the cause. For Niebuhr, these figures were always penultimate, that is to say, they always pointed beyond themselves, and the cause, to the One beyond the Many who is the author of all good causes.

All our marginalized responsibilists—Bishop Henry McNeal Turner, Ida B. Wells-Barnett, and Rev. Francis J. Grimké—fit this category. Their drive to sustain blacks and to reform their overall society was grounded in attempts to help others to meet their basic human needs, as well as successful efforts to realize fully their own humanity and full moral agency: this constituted their common cause. These selves were Christian selves; they specifically understood their cause as emanating from God, and through their accountability they were expressing the need, finally, to be reconciled with and before God. Their demands were provincially based but gave evidence of a universal reality: that all people were equally created by a God who loved them equally. Thus they can be rightfully considered to be transcendent selves in the cause of helping people meet their basic human needs, which is itself one of the causes, or projects, of God. It is a cause or project of God not simply because it is asserted as such by proponents of this position, such as this writer, but because it is phenomenologically manifested in creation and human community and is implied in major biblical themes and narratives.

We have followed this common thread—the commitment to helping people meet their basic human needs—as it was manifested in three responsible selves and have tried to analyze that thread in light of Niebuhrian categories and approaches. Obviously it cannot be said that the responsibilists were influenced by Niebuhr, nor can it be said that Niebuhr was aware of the ministry of these responsibilists. What has been demonstrated is the congruity between the ethical reflection and praxis of the responsibilists and Niebuhr's responsibilist ethic, although the congruity is not manifested in every regard, and, at least in some instances, it is manifested with some conceptual dissonance. Still, since these responsibilists predate Niebuhr and were not obscure, yet did not influence Niebuhr or other white ethicists of his generation, some explanation for the communication gap is in order.

White ethicists of Niebuhr's generation did not understand that these people were appropriate dialogue partners in a triadic moral relationship, and yet these selves were responsible selves. How could such responsible selves be ignored by people concerned with moral responsibility? The most obvious answer to this question is probably the correct one. Although nonmarginalized selves are aware of marginalized selves and Niebuhr felt substantial guilt over the hegemony whites enjoyed because of the color line, guilt does not make for true community or clear communication. Thus, although Niebuhr was clearly remorseful, he did not see the members of a debased community as sources of moral insight or as possible ethical dialogue partners. Traditionally, members of the underclass have been routinely infantilized while the benign powerful wrung their hands and bemoaned the process of marginalization and the malignant powerful refused to see the marginalized at all, since recognizing them would conflict with their efforts to marginalize. As a benign, empowered self, therefore, Niebuhr could not hear the cries of the oppressed of his generation, except as cries of suffering, but not as calls for dialogue. His social location made him socially deaf.

To a large extent, two or more systems of internal and external history obtain simultaneously in a society of oppression. We, the oppressed (at least some of us), regard Nat Turner, Denmark Vesey, Gabriel Prosser, David Walker, and John Brown as responsible selves, agents of God, who sought to help people meet their basic human needs for freedom, among other basic human needs. We are nevertheless aware of an external history as it was understood by the community of oppression, in which the aforementioned people were characterized as religious fanatics who sought to overthrow divinely sanctioned order. Although we understand the factual reality of this external history, we do not share in its perspective or in the sentiments expressed in it; for us, another history—an internal one—prevails.

Similarly, nonmarginalized selves, particularly to the extent that they are actively engaged in exploiting people and in denying them opportunities to realize their basic human needs, also have internal and external histories. Their internal history maintains that the American Indians relinquished their land in a fair exchange that introduced them to a "superior" culture and the technological benefits of that culture. Similarly, Africans were saved from their heathen ways by the introduction to Christianity, presumably a fair exchange for their enslavement. Transmitters of this tradition are memorialized, and critical accounts of it are not expected from domestic underlings, but only from foreign peers.[47] Thus the *homo responditus marginalis* (marginalized responding self) is seldom heard by his/her oppressor and all too often his/her message expressing suffering and demanding change goes unheeded. Whatever truth contained therein is lost until circumstances arise in which the oppressed become so active, so relentless, and so notorious that the world sees the interplay and comments critically on it. That is why the campaign against lynching that Ida B. Wells-Barnett waged in Great Britain was as important as the internationally televised civil rights demonstrations and freedom marches of the Martin Luther King, Jr., era. Yet, despite the suitability of a theology of meeting basic human needs as championed by marginalized responsibilists, even this approach has limitations and problematic applications. It is to these problems that we now turn.

Chapter 6

Facing the Inherent Limitations of Responsibility

The goal of this book has been achieved if we have provided better definition of Niebuhr's concept of appropriate response. This definition consists in our insistence upon the utilization of a "meeting of basic human needs approach" as a kind of middle axiom or as a general guideline for accounting for the divine initiative in the creation of human beings with attendant needs.[1] In accordance with this definition, it has also been suggested that the meeting of basic human needs constitutes a primary human response. These considerations serve as outermost guidelines for human praxis and ethical reflection, and as signposts indicating the turns that must be considered in making the most fitting response.

At no time should it be assumed, however, that the mere meeting of one's needs or the needs of others for whom one is responsible in itself constitutes action that is completely morally responsible. Similarly, the ethical reflection that precedes, is involved with, or follows such morally responsible action is also incomplete as a system of ethical reflection in the Christian social ethics tradition. It is further suggested, however, that the utilization of certain "meeting basic human needs considerations" can help responsibilists to critically assess the appropriate responses to a variety of circumstances and challenges. Helping people to meet their basic human needs and helping them to engage in the current political, economic, and social discourses on interpreting and satisfying needs in public debates also represents the kind of important moral interaction that keeps any Christian social ethic relevant, active, and challenged. In a world of scarcity, in countries that are differentiated, pluralistic, and characterized by many different organizations, ethnic groups, institutions, and communities, the obligation to create systems that help people meet their basic human needs is bound to keep an ethicist chastened as well as frequently perplexed.[2] The responsibilist approach appears to be efficacious in answering appropriately to a variety of responses from others, and this flexibility is of substantial importance. H. Richard Niebuhr is correct, however, when he maintains that there may be several approaches to solving moral problems: "And it is only an old, though deeply established, prejudice which will lead us to believe that there is only one fitting answer to the question, one ideal solution of the problem, one right relationship. 'God fulfills himself in many ways lest one good custom should corrupt the earth.'"[3]

The moral exemplars in this book were not selected because their approaches harmonize. On the contrary, they were chosen because, although they were roughly contemporaneous, they each had a distinct perspective, even though they were members of a common, oppressed African-American community. That each of their responses is morally justifiable is indeed suggestive of the truth that there is usually more than one appropriate response. Yet the common thread in their actions reveals that these actions and reflections did not simply constitute three approaches amid endless possibilities. The common thread consisted of their attempt, from a black Christian perspective, to help people in their marginalized communities meet one or more of their basic human needs without sacrificing their central basic human need for dignity. This commitment to self-respect did not allow them the option of letting themselves or their communities be treated as inferiors. It also forced them to resist the character assassination that was a common tool of oppression wielded against their marginalized communities.

This issue of self-esteem and self-regard, over time, constrained our responsibilists to criticize the redoubtable Booker T. Washington. They did so because, along with securing basic human needs for blacks, they insisted upon an immediate recognition of the basic worth and equality of blacks. In other words, they were never willing to secure the basic needs of blacks by compromising on this demand for the recognition of full humanity. Each exemplar understood that servility and rights claiming were incompatible responses in a modern, pluralistic nation in which membership and citizenship had been denied to African Americans. Each understood, in ways that Washington never publicly acknowledged, that to be whole, responsible selves required them to claim their full personhood and to oppose, or at least to criticize, those who would not recognize their equality.

It was not that Booker T. Washington was an irresponsible self so much as that he was a responsible self who did not fully understand the ultimate correlation between the task of securing all basic human needs and that of claiming full social recognition. Unfortunately, in his fight to help blacks secure several fundamental human needs, such as the acquisition of education, craft skills, entrepreneurial expertise, and property, he wrongfully relinquished claims for basic civil and political rights. This approach was internally contradictory and, not surprisingly, it undercut his provisional successes. At best, it was an approach that secured certain strategic advantages of no little value but that made for insufficient conditions for human flourishing. Yet Washington had noble motives, as Robert Michael Franklin shows in his sympathetic portrait:

> He adopted a publicly passive posture with respect to political participation and social integration with whites and identified the economic marketplace as the meaningful arena in which blacks might advance their cause without arousing the suspicions of whites. In his published private papers, however, Washington provided financial support for political and legal efforts to strike down discriminatory legislation and to increase black voter strength across the South.[4]

Franklin correctly points out that, in private, Washington was not the servile accommodationist one saw in public. He possessed basic integrity although he espoused a faulty, servile role playing for the black masses. His strategy required him to keep his "virility" and assertiveness private. If Washington's servile position had expressed his own personal relinquishment of his right to be appropriately regarded, one could hardly have criticized his posture. He would have been within his rights if he had exercised his own agency in that fashion. Since, however, he foreswore the recognition of full civil and political rights on behalf of the masses and in deference to oppressive white sensibilities, in the hopes of obtaining economic advancement, his approach was inherently defective and rightly criticized by our exemplars. Why this is so becomes apparent when we consider the case of Rev. George Liele, another responsibilist from an earlier era.

In colonial Virginia in 1751, Liele was born to slave parents, Liele and Nancy Sharpe. He served several masters and apparently adopted his father's first name as his last name. Around 1764, he was brought to the Savannah, Georgia, region by his master, Henry Sharpe. A very conscientious slave, Liele was soon converted to Christianity by a Reverend Mr. Moore, who also subsequently licensed him as a plantation missionary.

By August of 1777, Liele had obtained his freedom and organized a church in the vicinity of Savannah, Georgia. This church became one of the earliest independent black Baptist churches in America, and Liele was an extremely vigorous and successful minister. However, disaster soon struck in the form of the Revolutionary War. Since some of his family members were owned by Tories, Liele's church and clan obtained some protection when the British took Savannah in 1778, but as the war progressed, some of his patrons, such as Henry Sharpe, his former master, were killed. Finally, Loyalists were forced to leave the area, and Liele left with them.

At this point, Liele took superlative action on behalf of his marginalized community. Understanding that the greatest need of black people was to establish a religious base, Liele, a freeman, sold himself into indentured servitude to obtain passage to Jamaica. He wanted to preach the Gospel and establish a Baptist denomination there. By 1787, he had worked his way out of indentured servitude and had begun pastoring several churches. Of this experience he writes:

> I have deacons and elders, a few; and teachers of small congrega-
> tions in the town and country, where convenience suits them to come
> together; and I am pastor. I preach twice on the Lord's day, in the
> forenoon and afternoon, and twice in the week, and have not been
> absent six Sabbath days since I formed the church in this country. I
> receive nothing for my services; I preach, baptize, administer the
> Lord's Supper, and travel from one place to another to publish the
> gospel and to settle church affairs, all freely.[5]

Reading between the lines reveals that Liele was a responsible, marginalized self who took a servile role in order to help the people of his community, and to help those in Jamaica, a new mission field. He must have also thought that Jamaica was a viable mission field, which implied, in some fashion, that it also was a community toward which he felt some obligation, in the sense that he wanted to help in satisfying their basic human needs, the primary one being religion. In this small yet crucial way, Liele helped Jamaican slaves to begin to address all of their needs and to create a new basis for community, which was to take the place of their lost African heritage and community. For it is only by establishing a new community that any serious, effectual resistance to oppression emerges.[6] Thus Liele, and other men and women like him, acted and believed in ways that created the conditions whereby others might also begin to exercise serious and effectual moral agency.

Yet Liele was hardly a militant figure and did not advocate indentured servitude for all. He merely assumed for himself, in a supererogatory fashion, a superlative duty on behalf of others.[7] By viewing this task as a personal choice rather than presenting it as normative policy for the masses, he escapes the internal incoherence of Booker T. Washington's approach. Like our other responsibilists, Liele suffers; yet his suffering does not impugn his integrity. On the contrary, it is simply part of the existential experience inherent in the process of resisting oppression, and it culminates in the creation of a new community and a new, more fully realized Liele. In other words, Liele does not debase himself when he sacrifices for his communities of marginalization, but, much like Christ, with surprising kenotic effectiveness, he empties himself and subjects himself to debasement for the sake of others. Like Christ, Liele thus triumphs over forces of oppression and evil while not eliminating them from his setting. Although slavery was later outlawed in Jamaica, Liele did not live to see it. Just as Jesus of Nazareth struggled with the structural sin of the Roman empire but did not see ultimate triumph over sin within the time frame of his earthly ministry, so Liele's morally responsible actions were most fully enjoyed and realized by his posterity, both black and white.

In like fashion, modern responsible selves are called to oppose oppression, and this opposition is appropriate, or fitting, when it helps the agent and others for whom he/she acts to meet their basic human needs responsibly without sacrificing their sense of self-respect and self-esteem, especially when those acts also refrain from impugning the self-respect of others. At least on some occasions, such acts of intervention override the call and benefits of the "grace to do nothing." They also override mere militant posturing. These morally responsible acts are to be performed in humility, but with dignity. They constitute contributions to the cause of God; at least that is how they may be characterized by the Christian responsibilist.

INTERNATIONAL IMPLICATIONS AND LIMITATIONS

Helping people meet their own basic human needs is an appropriate commitment for every particular community that is capable of rendering aid. On an international scale, it also has moral ramifications for the recognition of other human communities, particularly by communities of great power and wealth. Indeed, why else would the West provide foreign humanitarian aid to the so-called Third World if it were not convinced that the destitute around the world help, in some fashion, to make up the species called human. To do nothing while others starve in Somalia or Ethiopia, when intervention is possible and the risks to would-be rescuers are relatively minimal, is inherently wrong from a number of moral viewpoints.

Yet if all people form one great human family, then all relations between international communities and states are subject to certain criteria of justice. In particular, there are issues of bargaining competency as regards commutative justice in the international economic marketplace. If, as certain writers assert, modern managerial, international economics invariably results in unfair exchanges that are detrimental to the common good of the human community, to the extent that weak traders are unable to meet their basic human needs, then some interventions are in order.[8] Accordingly, exchanges may have to be renegotiated and possibly loans may have to be forgiven or foreign aid advanced, not on the basis of charity but on the basis of a reparative justice that seeks to compensate for what must have been commutative injustice in previous economic exchanges.[9]

RESPONSIBLE SELVES IN A BELIEVING COMMUNITY

Our exemplars were moral paradigms precisely because they did not see themselves as merely individualistic selves. They did not regard themselves as risk-aversive calculators of interests who thought solely of themselves with reference to every moral dilemma or in every opportunity for advancement. Instead, they were irrevocably committed to their community, with the understanding that their own respective destinies would rise and fall with that of their community. As such, they fought for others as much as for themselves, if not more so. They lived lives that were clearly disadvantaged, compared to the standards of many of us in our own modern, pluralist, differentiated world. Yet they speak to us not out of a distant past, but out of a meaningful recent history. The struggle they waged has not ended here in the United States, let alone in other less fortunate and less naturally endowed places of the world.

William Julius Wilson's sociological study *The Truly Disadvantaged* suggests, among other things, that part of the problem facing the "truly disadvantaged" of our society lies in the paucity of appropriate role models available to them.[10] Wilson demonstrates statistically that with the death of Jim Crow, the creation of a black middle class, and the desegregation of numerous bedroom communities and suburbs, the underclass was abandoned by the middle class, which fled the troubled city for the greater economic advantages and comforts of the suburbs.[11] This abandonment has not merely been the product of white supremacy or managerial capitalism, but has also been a relinquishment by contemporary blacks of the kind of race patriotism featured so prominently by our exemplars. Stated bluntly, recent black strivers have left behind the inner city in the pursuit of the American Dream.

As a black man born into an inner city neighborhood in Newark, New Jersey, I have personally witnessed white flight and black abandonment. In the ghetto of my youth, there were indeed some whites and blacks who were not only able to meet their own basic human needs but were also able to help others. They did so for a variety of reasons, and their reasons and their examples enabled me, among many others, to establish a certain level of sustainability in this world, albeit poised ever so tentatively upon the thin ice of the white supremacy that still prevails in America. Nevertheless, in my experience, some of the most morally impressive people were those who could have left the troubles of the ghettoes, the crime, the drugs, the chronic unemployment, the oppression of slum housing, yet chose not to do so, so that they might help others. Their proximity to the truly disadvantaged allowed them to aid others while also allowing them to serve as role models. Logically speaking, the self-imposed duty of forming solidarity with the truly disadvantaged must be a part of any viable responsibilist ethics.

If churches will not create any community movements of solidarity, others will. If some Christians will not take on the yoke of Jesus and stand in solidarity with the poor, then at least one project of God will be left undone or will be fulfilled by someone appointed by God who does God's will on Earth as it is in heaven from some community other than the one that calls itself the church. And it will be done by people who are not commonly called Christian.

An incarnational approach, like that of Eugene Lang—the famous industrialist who committed both himself and his resources to his elementary school alma mater and its current graduates—would seem to be required from at least some empowered selves.[12] And also from some marginalized selves.

This study has been conducted primarily for the benefit of African Americans—those who are provisionally secure and skate on the thin ice of a white supremacist America that accepts our labor and love while refusing to fully acknowledge our worth. Yet it is not meant to be exclusive; let anyone who has ears to hear, hear! Empowered selves can stand in solidarity with the oppressed; yet to do so will bring them into conflict with oppressive forces that are dedicated to maintaining an oppressive status quo. As empowered or marginalized Christians, our loyalties lie with the One beyond the Many, who calls us to love each other as Christ loved the church. This call is not race, sex, or class specific, although its answer must, in some respects, be color, sex, and class specific. As a man I can write about responsibilist womanists such as Ida Wells-Barnett, but I cannot speak for womanists. I can work in solidarity with the destitute but not deem myself their spokesperson. Similarly, others can work in solidarity with the homeless without engaging in the impulse to explain them away, or to infantilize them by providing everything for them. Whites who dare to stand in solidarity with oppressed blacks cannot be their spokespeople, except as they are assigned that task and designation by blacks. Such a new praxis requires a different form of leadership and different sorts of moral agents. Servant-leaders who can remove obstacles rather than direct traffic seem to be the most appropriate models, as becomes apparent from a reconsideration of our exemplars.

The leadership of our responsibilists was most impressive when it was an inspired, enabling leadership. This style allowed the downtrodden to make their own claims and to assert their own humanity. When this approach is used, the truly disadvantaged are able to see the dignity in themselves, and they are able to claim a proper and rightful recognition of it. In this way, all persons within the territorial boundaries of a designated community realize themselves more fully as morally competent human beings and recognize their capacities more easily. All people become more fully human thereby. Oppressors are able to become more fully human by listening and hearing the cries of the oppressed, and, like Lazarus the tax collector, they can then begin the process of repentance and reparative justice that allows them to reclaim the humanity from which their acts of oppression had alienated them. Empowered selves previously guilty of sins of omission realize themselves more fully by abandoning their dereliction of duty and taking on the yoke of Christ. Marginalized selves realize their fullest humanity in resisting oppression and in meeting their own basic needs and those of others. In so doing, they, like George Liele, act as fully competent moral agents, although they may never obtain a full recognition of their humanity from their oppressors. They know, and their community knows, who they are and whose they are. Most important, God knows who they are and accepts all who will come and attend to one of God's many projects.

CONCLUSION

This study concludes where it began, with a realization that we live in a world of oppression. We are constrained to ask, as did Niebuhr, "What is going on?" We must also ask, "What is God doing?" We discover the answers to these provocative questions by looking at the world and by living in it in solidarity with its oppressed people. We are compelled to listen to each other, and to participate dialectically in what Paulo Freire calls the process of "conscientization"—escaping cultural invasion.[13] Barriers of self-interest that go beyond basic needs can be recognized if we listen. And with recognition, their removal becomes possible.

Finally, it must be recognized that the answers to the aforementioned foundational questions will only be discovered and realized in the common struggle with marginalized people in the quest to meet basic human needs. This work is a confession that the struggle can and should be joined from a Christian perspective and, most specifically, but not exclusively, from the black church experience. Yet it must also be confessed that this struggle is God's and not the possession of any one community. Thus as circumstances arise, alliances must be made and kept with Christians who have different internal histories as well as with non-Christians dedicated to helping all people to meet their basic human needs.

Delicate Alliances—Conflicting Motivations and "Fitting Acts"

One of the major limitations of the approach we have been discussing becomes clear when we work with marginalized others who need help, but whose inner histories do not allow provision of any but the most limited assistance. It is therefore inappropriate to assist others in fulfilling what the assistant believes to be a basic human need when it is not seen as such by the would-be beneficiary of the assistance, the putative marginalized person. Such inappropriate aid invariably impugns the integrity and conscience of the marginalized person or community and does more harm than good to the ongoing moral interactions. One example is the defense of pacifists by the use of violent force. Another is the provision of inappropriate nourishment, as when forbidden foods are fed to Muslims. Still another example is aid given to black Christians in the guise of racist ideology and action.[1] These attempts, no matter how well intended, invariably result in some form of moral imperialism. Thus, would-be responsibilists must always be careful to assist others rather than to control or to impose upon them. If it is to have any positive moral value, aid must be recognized by the oppressed as aid.

Yet, when aid is obviously desired—as when Jesus healed a man on the Sabbath, a time customarily designated for rest—the assistance can be tendered in an appropriate fashion that glorifies God and fulfills a part of the divine projects. However, the rendering of aid in inappropriate fashion will require that people communicate with each other in clearer and truer modes than heretofore. This is where the genius of Niebuhr's approach to Christian social ethics comes in: the commitment to ongoing conversation, phenom-enological observation, action in and relation to a community, and an ongoing relationship with a God who is immanent to all of the dialogue partners but who is also transcendent to them.

This God is able to relate to those who would follow God on a permanent basis and is able to help those who would help the helpless on God's behalf. This God is in the process of aiding people who will not read this book and who have not yet entered into conversation with this author. It is part of the new responsibilities of post-Niebuhrian responsibilists to discover anew the silenced voices, the new disenfranchised ones that every generation of humanity spawns.[2] This task is a never-ending task, for no utopia can be created, and the most important conversations and projects are never finished. The responsibilist in the marginalized community has the task of discovering how he/she contributes to the process of marginalization and how that contribution can be ended and replaced by an approach that helps people to meet their basic human needs while recognizing their basic human dignity. Let us all continue to do the fitting thing, and let us all hear the voices of the silenced.

Notes

INTRODUCTION

1. H. Richard Niebuhr, *The Responsible Self* (New York: Harper & Row, 1963), 126.

2. The answer offered herein is only secondarily concerned with the theodicy problem that the inquiry posed presents and will address that issue only as an ancillary concern. It does not seek to illuminate why bad things happen to good people so much as to explore the moral obligations of Christians who seek the "fitting" response in a world in which evil is frequently manifested.

3. James W. Fowler, an insightful critic of Niebuhr notes: "For Niebuhr, I suspect, the reality of the Center of radically monotheistic faith was so real and vivid that the ethics of response to that One's being, valuing, and faithfulness seemed to have sufficient normative determinateness. Such faith can be trusted to know and do the 'fitting' thing. Therefore it was not necessary to develop guidelines or 'middle axioms' or other heuristic devices for use as aids (and checks) in the process of ethical discernment. Here a theological ethics, grounded in faith in the objectivity and reality of God, places excessive trust in the human subjective perception of and response to that God. For that reason it fails to adequately address the need for determinate specifications of ethical imperatives for concrete situations" (*To See the Kingdom: The Theological Vision of H. Richard Niebuhr* [Nashville: Abingdon Press, 1974], 264). Joseph L. Allen, observes: "What for Niebuhr would make an action fitting rather than unfitting? His answers to this question, though valid as far as they go, are very general and not fully satisfactory" (*Love and Conflict* [Nashville: Abingdon Press, 1984], 54).

4. Jesus of Nazareth effectively illustrates the moral competence of "evil" people in Matthew 7:9–11, observing: "Is there anyone among you who, if your

child asks for bread, will give a stone? Or if the child asks for a fish, will give a snake? If you, then, who are evil, know how to give good gifts to your children, how much more will your Father in heaven give good things to those who ask him!"

5. Julio De Santa Ana, *Towards a Church of the Poor: The Work of an Ecumenical Group on the Church and the Poor* (New York: Orbis Press, 1981), 22, 23.

6. Gustavo Gutiérrez, *The Power of the Poor in History,* trans. Robert Barr (Maryknoll, N.Y.: Orbis Press, 1984), 193.

7. Katie G. Cannon, *Black Womanist Ethics* (Atlanta: Scholars Press, 1988), 67.

8. The best description of working-class marginalization has come from Cornel West, who writes: "The circumstances of the black poor and those for the black working class (including both blue- and white-collar workers) are qualitatively similar and only quantitatively different. In other words, the Afro-American working class merely (yet significantly, in human terms) have higher-paying jobs than the Afro-American lower class; but neither have any meaningful participation in the decision-making process as to who gets hired or fired, nor any control over the production of goods and services" (*Prophesy Deliverance! An Afro-American Revolutionary Christianity* [Philadelphia: Westminster Press, 1982], 89, 90).

9. The classic example of this process is Pontius Pilate, who literally and figuratively washes his hands of his political responsibility to administer justice for Jesus of Nazareth.

10. By preferential option for the poor I refer to the action of God on behalf of oppressed people. A Latin American theologian, Ronaldo Muñoz, expresses it well as follows: "Jesus' God is not the god of the ruling powers, not the 'almighty' evoked and invoked by the powerful of this world, but precisely the opposite. His is the God who comes to reign, whose will is to be done . . . from the side of the weak, lifting up the downtrodden, setting captives free. . . . The God of the Kingdom who comes with Jesus is none other than the Father, who comes to give us life and dignity, beginning with the most deprived: who commits us to following Jesus in his task of liberating the oppressed and by way of humble service" (*The God of Christians,* trans. Paul Burns [Maryknoll, N.Y.: Orbis Books, 1990], 144). I, of course, understand "the poor" in this sense to be all oppressed people, not just those economically oppressed.

11. If the marginalized or their allies in solidarity are convinced that God works in the world to convert culture, then they should share H. Richard Niebuhr's conversionist sentiments. Niebuhr writes: "The conversionist, with his view of history as the present encounter with God in Christ, does not live so much in expectation of a final ending of the world of creation and culture as in awareness of the power of the Lord to transform all things by lifting them up to himself. His imagery is spatial and not temporal; and the movement of life he finds to be issuing from Jesus Christ is an upward movement, the rising of men's soul's and deeds and thoughts in a mighty surge of adoration and glorification of the One who draws them to himself. This is what human culture can be—a transformed human life in and to the glory of God" (*Christ and Culture* [New York: Harper & Row, 1975], 195,

196). Besides changing culture, this same Christ can change all social structures and can call all disciples to attend to the duties that are necessary for the transformation.

12.   Indeed, this is the cause that could rightfully claim our loyalty, not because of devotion to a class, such as the vulgar communist devotion to the proletariat, but rather as an expression of loyalty to God. H. Richard Niebuhr wrote of loyalty in relation to the work of Christian philosopher, Josiah Royce: "Moral maturity comes when individual self-will gives way to a loyalty that, freely choosing a larger cause, unifies self and world in its service. 'A loyal man is one who has found and who sees, neither mere individual fellowmen to be loved or hated, nor mere conventions nor customs, nor laws to be obeyed, but some social cause or system of causes, so rich, so well-knit, and, to him, so fascinating and withal so kindly in its appeal to his natural self-will, that he says to his cause: "Thy will is mine and mine is thine. In thee I do not lose but find myself living intensely in proportion as I live for thee" ' " (*Radical Monotheism and Western Culture* [New York: Harper & Row, 1970], 21–22). For many Christians, moral maturity is demonstrated in voluntarily coming into solidarity with the oppressed.

13.   I agree with James Cone when he says that formalized training is not the primary criterion for enabling one to reflect ethically. Thus I also agree with his assertion that moral exemplars from various sources may be safely relied upon. Cone puts it this way: "We must not be afraid to call on the 'black and unknown bards of long ago' who created ethical patterns of behavior in song and story as they accepted the risks to fight for freedom. Their words may not be neatly structured to command the interests of white ethicists at Harvard Divinity School or Union Theological Seminary. But their truth is contained in the living reality of black people and not in philosophical and theological textbooks. . . . We must take these black realities and place them alongside biblical revelation, and then ask, 'What are we black people to do?' " (*God of the Oppressed* [New York: Seabury Press, 1975], 206).

14.   Paulo Freire, *Pedagogy of the Oppressed*, trans. Myra Bergman Ramos (New York: Seabury Press, 1970), 34, 35.

15.   The formative nature of Niebuhr's work, and the need for a further development of it, has been brought to my attention by E. Clinton Gardner, an ethicist who has contributed to that development over a number of years.

16.   Niebuhr's inquiring selves tend to be powerful selves. He writes: "We reinterpret our future also as we identify ourselves with different groups" (*The Responsible Self*, 105). He then gives two examples; one is an industrialist and the other is a statesman. Absent from these examples is the homeless vagrant or share-cropper, who also engage in reinterpretation.

17.   In some respects, this book is an attempt to move from what Enoch Oglesby, a noted black ethicist, has characterized as an "unstructured ethic of responsibility . . . described in the Black Church as 'keeping-the-charge,' " to what he has called a "more 'structured' or theoretical understanding of the idea of responsibility in theological discourse vis-a-vis the black struggle" (*Ethics and Theology from the other Side: Sounds of Moral Struggle* [Lanham, Md.: University Press of

America, 1979], 150–51). Oglesby concludes: "If our current analysis bears any legitimate weight at all relative to the black liberation struggle, it is that the use of the symbolism of responsibility in ethics and Black Theology must be one of the ground rules for moral action on the part of the oppressed. The symbol of responsibility means that the oppressed themselves must begin to appropriate their struggle in a different light. What I am suggesting here is that the oppressed must not think of themselves as 'helpless victims' but as *aggressive-responsive beings,* capable of responding in a creative way to the multifaceted realities of the black condition in American society" (ibid., 151–52).

CHAPTER 1. THE "RESPONSIBLE SELF": WHO IS HE/SHE?

1.   William Julius Wilson, *The Truly Disadvantaged* (Chicago: University of Chicago Press, 1987), 6–8.

2.   Fowler, *To See the Kingdom,* 5.

3.   Justus D. Doenecke, a Catholic scholar, writes: "In 1922 he [Niebuhr] stressed the higher righteousness of the Sermon on the Mount, the coming Kingdom of God on earth, and such parables of ethics as the Good Samaritan and Dives and Lazarus. At the same time, he protested against the exploitation of workers, sought legislation to protect the rights of women and children, and called for greater economic equality" ("H. Richard Niebuhr: Critic of Political Theology," *Communio* 4 [Spring 1977], 84, 85).

4.   Niebuhr, *Christ and Culture,* 233.

5.   Niebuhr, *Responsible Self,* 45.

6.   Ibid., 160. The Latin terms are used in order to avoid noninclusive language such as man-the-maker and similar expressions.

7.   Ibid., chap. 1, "The Meaning of Responsibility," 47–68.

8.   "It is, rather, the acknowledgment of my existence as the counterpart of another self. The exploration of this dimension of self-existence has taken place in many areas of modern man's thinking; many lines of inquiry have converged on the recognition that the self is fundamentally social, in this sense that it is a being which not only knows itself in relation to other selves but exists as self only in that relation" (ibid., 71).

9.   "When we think of the relations of managers and employees we do not simply ask about the ends each group is consciously pursuing nor about the self-legislated laws they are obeying but about the way they are responding to each other's actions in accordance with their interpretations" (ibid., 62).

10.   Ibid., 92, 93.

11.   H. Richard Niebuhr, *The Meaning of Revelation* (New York: Macmillan, 1960), 83.

12.   Niebuhr, *Responsible Self,* 1.

13.   It is not unreasonable to suggest that Niebuhr's position logically demands the adoption of such an option.

14. "Responsibility lies in the agent who stays with his action, who accepts the consequences in the form of reactions and looks forward in a present deed to the continued interaction" (ibid., 64).

15. Of course, Niebuhr was well aware of the fact that there are conflicting groups in society that can call into account responsible selves in a variety of ways and to varying degrees of commitment.

16. For a classic statement on the issue of systematically distorted communication, see Jurgen Habermas's *Communication and the Evolution of Society* (Boston: Beacon Press, 1979), 209, 210.

17. See H. Richard Niebuhr's perceptive study, "Denominationalism and the Color Line," in *The Social Sources of Denominationalism* (New York: New American Library, 1957), 236–64.

18. Ibid., 254.

19. "Finally, the schism of the racial churches was and remains due to the difference in the culture levels of the two races. The Negroes, like the disinherited, required an emotional, empirical religion. 'The heart depressed by drudgery, hardship, forlornness craves not merely moral guidance but exhilaration and ecstasy.' Emotionalism in religion, however, was not only a reaction against the monotony and misery of laborious days on the plantation or in the factory, it was also the natural result of America's failure to provide the Negro with those educational opportunities which have brought about great changes in the religion of the disinherited and of the frontier" (ibid., 262). Niebuhr is completely unaware here of his own cultural imperialism and relativism, which accounts for the perception that emotionalism is primitive. Furthermore, his lack of appreciation of African-American culture is obvious. Despite his own cultural bias, Niebuhr was shrewd enough to note that Negroes were becoming better educated in his era, but cultural and economic equivalency would not generate full acceptance and equality. He notes: "But the cultural rise of the Negro holds out little hope for the unification of his churches with those of his whilom masters. Something more than a sociological cure seems necessary for the healing of this wound in the body of Christ" (ibid., 263). Nevertheless, Niebuhr never did suggest what an actual cure might look like from a praxeological standpoint.

20. During most of the years that Niebuhr wrote—beginning with *Social Sources of Denominationalism* and ending with his posthumously published *Responsible Self*—African Americans fought de jure segregation. George D. Kelsey's remarks express the feelings of most blacks of his era: "Segregation may be defined as 'the enforced separation of racial groups, either in regard to a few areas for life or in regard to many or all.' In the Southern United States the enforced separation of the races has traditionally been made in all areas of life. In the definition of segregation, the word 'enforced' must be given as much emphasis as the word 'separation.' Contrary to much popular opinion and especially the opinion of those who defend the system, segregation is not the expression of a social contract. It is not a covenant entered into by black and white people in a cool hour of reflection. It is not an agreement

worked out in the interest of the smoothest possible functioning of society. Segregation is a hostile and contemptuous thrust of power by the strong. It is the product of a unilateral decision made by the dominant group alone, which aims precisely at the maintenance of an order of superordination and subordination" (*Racism and the Christian Understanding of Man* [New York: Charles Scribner's Sons, 1965], 97–98). Concerning segregation in the churches of this era, E. Clinton Gardner wrote: "The churches themselves generally followed the patterns of segregation in the community at large, and hence came to be racially exclusive. Sometimes this exclusiveness of the churches was the result of the Negroes *being forced out* of the white churches; more frequently it was the result of the Negroes' withdrawal in order to escape *the inferior status* which they had in the predominately white churches. This pattern has persisted on down to the present with relatively slight modification" (*Biblical Faith and Social Ethics* [New York: Harper & Brothers, 1960], 344; emphasis added). Although some blacks of this era, in particular Marcus Garvey and Elijah Muhammad, favored the voluntary separation of blacks and whites, these leaders never represented the vast majority of black public opinion. Most blacks understood segregation to be a form of oppression.

21.   Niebuhr, *Responsible Self*, 158.

22.   E. Clinton Gardner, "Responsibility and Moral Direction in the Ethics of H. Richard Niebuhr," *Encounter* 40, no. 2 (Spring 1979): 143–68.

23.   Niebuhr, *Meaning of Revelation*, 113.

24.   Niebuhr writes: "In whatever form we interpret Christian ethics, in it Christ always has something of this double character. In him man is directed toward God; in him also God is directed toward men" (*Responsible Self*, 163).

25.   Ibid., 158.

26.   Ibid., 164.

27.   See Fowler, *To See the Kingdom*, 89. The quote is taken from a paper by Niebuhr that was entitled, "The Social Gospel and the Mind of Jesus," which he delivered on April 21, 1933, at a meeting of the American Theological Society in New York.

28.   Indeed, Doenecke considers Niebuhr a stringent critic of political theologies. If Doenecke is correct, Niebuhr's work grows ever more relevant and problematic as theologies become more aware of and engage in dialogue with modern political thought. See his "H. Richard Niebuhr," 83–93.

29.   Niebuhr, *Responsible Self*, 164, 165. The major problem with this quote is Niebuhr's failure to distinguish between natural action and social action. God wills rain in a different and more direct fashion than God wills the abuse of authority by political powers. At least that is what will be argued for here. Niebuhr appears to equate the two circumstances, and this equation is a fundamental mistake.

30.   James Fowler notes: "In a mind as attuned to polarities in existence as Niebuhr's, and as sensitive as he was to nuances of self-centeredness in the most altruistic of motivations, the appropriate response to all but the most heinous of abuses of companions seemed to be expectant waiting, and suffering if necessary. Just as in his theology the word God has no unqualified predicate, so in his ethics

the *will* or *action of God* can have no unqualified specificity. This is the most serious limitation of an ethics that is deeply and consistently Christlike" (*To See the Kingdom*, 265). Romney Moseley is also critical about this aspect of Niebuhr's work: "Niebuhr prophetically calls human beings to respond to their true vocation as trustworthy and loyal participants in a triadic covenant that was initiated by God, the Creator, Governor, and Redeemer. His images of the human as *Homo dialogicus* and *Homo poeta* presume that social harmony will triumph over chaos and that God's presence in Jesus the Christ inspires us to recognize that authentic selfhood is constituted only in relation to an ever-widening nexus of moral relationships and responsibilities. While I find some consolation in Niebuhr's optimistic belief that all things come together in a coherent universe under the sovereignty of God, I must question this theological anthropology from the perspective of the moral imperative for solidarity with victims of oppression throughout the world. Niebuhr read history through the eyes of American pragmatism and progressivism. He believed that meaning could arise from social interaction and that normative 'I-Thou' relationships are possible. The principal threats to social harmony are 'chaotic pluralism' and its accompanying moral relativism. Those for whom the historical basis of faith is the underside of history cannot be so optimistic about faith on earth. For them the threat to the quest for meaning is, undoubtedly, the history of human suffering. Suffering ruptures the flow of progressivist theology and psychology. Suffering is the arena in which we are radically challenged to make sense of what it means to be human, what it means to be authentic selves before God" (*Becoming a Self before God: Critical Transformations* [Nashville: Abingdon Press, 1991], 69).

31.   W. E. B. Du Bois, *W. E. B. Du Bois Speaks, 1890–1919*, 2 vols., ed. Philip Foner, (New York: Pathfinder Press, 1970), 1:79; emphasis added.

32.   W. E. B. Du Bois, *The Souls of Black Folk* (New York: Signet Classics, New American Library, 1969), 54. The paradoxical should again be noted in that Du Bois himself was a male chauvinist and frequently denied black women equal opportunity to work to their fullest ability in resisting white supremacy (see Cannon, *Black Womanist Ethics*, 108). For a presentation of Du Bois as a sensitive ally of women in their struggle for equality, see Manning Marable, *How Capitalism Underdeveloped Black America: Problems in Race, Political Economy and Society* (Boston: South End Press, 1983), 82–84; emphasis added.

33.   Niebuhr, *Responsible Self*, 60.

34.   James Cone has much more insight than Niebuhr does into both the relationship between suffering and oppression and the differences between them. He writes: "The question about the human person is not answered by enumerating a list of properties; a person is not a collection of properties that can be scientifically analyzed. Rather to speak of the human being is to speak about its being-in-the-world-of-human-oppression. With the reality of human suffering as our starting point, what can black theology say about human nature?" (*A Black Theology of Liberation* [Maryknoll, N.Y.: Orbis Press, 1990], 87).

35.   Niebuhr, *Responsible Self*, 60.

36.   Cone, *Black Theology*, 89.

37. Niebuhr, *Meaning of Revelation,* 5, 6.

38. Cone writes: "Without minimizing the horror of social, economic, and political losses, it may at least be noted that these are expected by the oppressed, and that one's life can be adjusted to accommodate physical pain. It is not possible to be black and not know what white people do to black people" (*Black Theology,* 98).

39. Ibid., 103.

40. The social location of an ethical agent is important although not determinative. José Míguez Bonino has a clear way of making this point: "A social location determines a perspective. It conceals some things and reveals others. We have sometimes referred to this in terms of 'the epistemological privilege of the poor.' The poor are not morally or spiritually superior to others, but they do see reality from a different angle or location—and therefore differently" (*Toward a Christian Political Ethics* [Philadelphia: Fortress Press, 1983], 43). It is maintained in the present work that oppressed people do not possess a superior human nature, but a more useful social and psychological location than oppressors. This advantage allows some of them to achieve a keener interpretation of the Bible and the requirements of human obligation.

41. Cone, *Black Theology,* 80, 81.

42. Ibid., 72, 73.

43. Cone, *God of the Oppressed,* 89, 90.

44. In fairness to Niebuhr, it can be said that he is not diametrically opposed to all interventions, whereas he is diametrically opposed to the usurpation of the divine initiative by self-righteous reformers. Niebuhr has maintained that "there is indeed no room for self-appointed avengers and Messiahs. 'Vengeance is mine' says this Lord. But neither is passive waiting possible. Activity is inescapable. The only activity which man cannot exert is God's activity. But he cannot evade the necessity of acting in the interim before the judgment, of preparing for death and for life. . . . This day the Lord set life and death before him. Such interim ethics are not the ethics of quiescence. Precisely because God is moving man cannot sit still" ("The Social Gospel and the Mind of Jesus," as quoted in James Fowler's *To See the Kingdom,* 92). Unfortunately, it is at this very point that Niebuhr fails to give any indication of what kinds of action other than repentance would qualify as fitting responses. It may well be that he wanted to be more instructive as to what might constitute fitting responses in a subsequent book. His untimely death, however, prevented him from completing such a task. Nevertheless, he maintains in his manuscript that responsible selves do participate in the activities of God. They do so, not because they perfectly understand the will of God. Rather they do so as repentant, loyal, fallible, agents of God, seeking to discern the continued will of God through their actions made in faith rather than in certainty.

45. See Gardner, "Ethics of H. Richard Niebuhr," 164.

46. Universal loyalty refers to Niebuhr's understanding of an ongoing moral community that includes all people without regard to their own religious, ethical, or political beliefs and practices. Of universality, Niebuhr writes: "Christianity has been marked by the passion for universality. It understands that faith in God cannot

become incarnate except in a universal community in which all walls of partition have been broken down. Through Jesus Christ sinners as well as righteous, Gentiles as well as Jews, and the dead as well as the living have been given and are to be given access in faith to the one Father, and by him they are called to loyalty to the one kingdom. The drive to universality has been present in Christianity from the beginning; it has been expressed in its expansive and missionary movements as well as in its efforts to maintain a catholic church" (*Radical Monotheism*, 62).

47.   Such a pronouncement would be, however, a far cry from what Niebuhr himself did. Niebuhr writes, "The causes for which we live all die. The great social movements are supplanted by others. The ideals we fashion are revealed by time to be relative. The empires and cities to which we are devoted all decay. At the end nothing is left to defend us against the void of meaninglessness" (ibid., 122). Thus a liberationist intent on retaining some sort of Niebuhrian orientation might insist that social solidarity with the poor is the cause of God, rather than the cause of the poor themselves as a social class.

48.   H. Richard Niebuhr, "The Grace of Doing Nothing," *The Christian Century* 49 (23 March 1932), 378–80.

49.   Ibid., 380.

50.   I do not mean to imply that Niebuhr was an isolationist or a pacifist, but rather that he was annoyed with do-gooders who were totally unaware of their own foibles, faults, and limited moral capacities.

51.   John Kelly, "Time for the Grace of Doing Nothing," *The Christian Century* 105, no. 31 (26 Oct. 1988), 940.

52.   Niebuhr notes: "The Christian reflects upon the fact that his inability to do anything constructive in the crisis is the inability of one whose own faults are so apparent and so similar to those of the offender, that any action on his part is not only likely to be misinterpreted but is also likely . . . to be really less than disinterested" ("The Grace of Doing Nothing," 379). Niebuhr also noted elsewhere, "What is fitting, useful, and complementary to an existence can be determined only if disinterestedness, or abstraction from desire, is practiced and the nature and tendency of the being in question are studied" (*Radical Monotheism*, 103). This last remark appears to endorse the pursuit of disinterestedness, or ideal objectivity, as a desirable state of mind for engaging in moral reflection. Such a point of view contradicts modern liberationist approaches that employ a hermeneutics of suspicion to all moral reasoning, including our own, based upon the realization that no individual or group is perfectly disinterested, and therefore ethical deliberations have to take into consideration the reality of bias and the commitment to individual and group interests. Since Niebuhr was aware that no individual or group could be absolutely disinterested, his call for attempts to attain disinterestedness is problematic. It is possible, however, that Niebuhr believed we should strive for pure objectivity, even as we are aware that we cannot arrive at that state.

53.   The ethical quality of the moral actor's motivations merely makes up one factor to consider in regard to the rightness of possible interventions or the refusal to intervene.

54.   Carlyle F. Stewart III considers the ethics of both Niebuhr and Cone to be ethically relative, that is to say, both approaches are explicitly conditional by the socially conditioned mores of the respective authors. Construing Cone's approach in Niebuhrian terms, he writes: "For Cone, then, liberation is a 'fitting response' to oppression and dehumanization, and since what is ethically good for oppressors (maintaining the status quo) is bad for the oppressed, his ethics is equally relativistic. Because of the relative nature of ethical judgments, Cone sees no reason why the oppressed in their struggle for freedom cannot formulate ethical principles in accordance with their own conception of the good and right" (*God, Being and Liberation: A Comparative Analysis of the Theologies and Ethics of James H. Cone and Howard Thurman* [Lanham, Md.: University Press of America, 1989], 224).

55.   From "The Negro and His Citizenship," in *The Works of Francis J. Grimké: Addresses Mainly Personal and Racial*, ed. Carter G. Woodson, vol. 1 (Washington, D.C.: Associated Publishers, 1942), 404.

56.   It is an awareness of this double consciousness—of being a victim and a victimizer—that gives the responsible marginalized self the possibility of avoiding the hubris that offended Niebuhr.

57.   Even the apostle Paul is aware of the struggles that the self undergoes in doing the right thing. Paul acknowledges his double consciousness in relation to divine law and human sin in Rom. 7:18–24: "I know that nothing good lives in me, that is, in my sinful nature. For what I do is not the good I want to do; no, the evil I do not want to do—this I keep on doing. Now if I do what I do not want to do, it is no longer I who do it, but it is sin living in me that does it. So I find this law at work: When I want to do good, evil is right there with me. For in my inner being I delight in God's law; but I see another law at work in the members of my body, waging war against the law of my mind and making me a prisoner of the law of sin at work within my members. What a wretched man I am!" (New International Version, Interlinear Greek-English New Testament [Grand Rapids, Mich.: Zondervan, 1980]). To say that one is oppressed does not exclude one from being rightfully designated as an oppressor by a victim of one's oppression in another community or context.

CHAPTER 2. BISHOP HENRY MCNEAL TURNER: RESPONSIBLE REPATRIATION

1.   Marable, *Capitalism*, 70–71.

2.   For an insightful study on the difficulty of practicing one's religion during this period, see Albert Raboteau, *Slave Religion* (New York: Oxford University Press, 1978).

3.   Gayraud Wilmore writes: "In addition to intimidation and murder, the so-called redeemers of the South, relieved of the presence of federal troops in 1877 and encouraged by northern complacency, began to use chicanery and economic reprisals against defenseless black landowners and tenant farmers. The situation in the North was not much better. White industrial workers resented the rising demand of blacks for jobs and equal rights and violently resisted the threat that the

unemployed posed for the lily-white trade unions (*Black Religion and Black Radicalism: An Interpretation of the Religious History of Afro-American People* [Maryknoll, N.Y.: Orbis Books, 1989], 139).

4.   Katie Cannon describes well the process of marginalization that took place during Reconstruction: "Fearful of the emerging competitive race relations with Blacks, white America instituted a whole set of statutes, ordinances, policies and customs in order to maintain white supremacy and to further white privileges in the areas of education, politics and economics. Whites wanted to regulate and eventually stamp out all notions of social equality between the races. Terror of Black encroachment in areas where whites claimed power and privileges even caused southern state legislatures to enact 'Black Codes,' similar to slave codes, designed to limit drastically the rights of ex-slaves. 'Although their provisions varied among states, the Black Codes essentially prevented the freedmen from voting or holding office, made them ineligible for military service, and disbarred them from serving on juries or testifying in court against whites. Moreover, blacks were forbidden to travel from place to place without passes, were not allowed to assemble without a formal permit from authorities, and could be fined and bound out to labor contractors if they were unwilling to work'" (*Black Womanist Ethics*, 49).

5.   Marable, *Capitalism*, 115.

6.   According to one recent biographer, Turner sometimes claimed an earlier birth date for strategic purposes related to his ordination. See the noted Turner biographer, Stephen Ward Angell, *Bishop Henry McNeal Turner and African-American Religion in the South* (Knoxville: University of Tennessee Press, 1992), 278 n. 1.

7.   Ibid., 8.

8.   Ibid., 12.

9.   Even Booker T. Washington, who was estranged from Turner in their later years, admitted the great usefulness of Turner's service: "It was in the establishing of Churches throughout Georgia . . . that he rendered the South a signal service. . . . These Churches were . . . the Negro's first social centers; their organization for general uplift . . . the very large part which Bishop Turner had in laying these foundations makes him worthy of being classed as a useful citizen in its largest sense (quoted in Angell, *Bishop Henry McNeal Turner,* 249).

10.   Edwin S. Redkey, ed., *Respect Black: The Writings and Speeches of Henry McNeal Turner* (New York: Arno Press, 1971), 74.

11.   Ibid.

12.   Ibid.

13.   Turner writes: "Men talk about evolution, but here is to be evolution in its fullest grandeur. God intends that his degraded race, which has been dwarfed through ages of heathenism, shall imbibe your civilization with its religion, and when sufficiently sobered through generations of self-possession, return to Africa and bring its millions to Christ and heaven" (ibid., 74).

14.   Turner's views on the social status of women was relatively radical for his era. Unlike nearly all of his contemporary male A.M.E. ministers, he supported

the ordination of women and expanded leadership roles for them in the church. He went so far as to ordain Sarah Ann Hughes, a highly competent woman, who had been divested of a pastorate in North Carolina by sexist reactionaries. Unfortunately, Turner did not justify his actions well, and although he never abandoned her cause, he was nonetheless unable to prevent Hughes's subsequent defrocking. For a full account of this matter, see Angell, *Bishop Henry McNeal Turner*, 181–84. Turner was also a supporter of radical women who were "race patriots," such as Ida Wells-Barnett.

15.   Stephen Angell maintains that Turner's commitment to self-segregation was gradual and incremental. He notes that Turner initially agreed with certain accommodationists: "James Lynch, an A.M.E. minister and a friend of Turner's, was a persistent advocate of the idea that blacks should assimilate wholly into one large American nation. He especially wanted to eliminate 'African' from the name of the A.M.E. Church, later acting on this conviction by switching his membership to the M.E. Church. Surprisingly, Turner on occasion agreed with some of Lynch's stands. In 1864, Turner was willing to have the word 'African' replaced by 'Allen' in the name of the denomination, thus preserving the church's initials and advertising the openness of the church to white membership" (*Bishop Henry Mc-Neal Turner*, 48).

16.   Redkey, *Respect Black*, 14–16.

17.   Turner writes: "God saw fit to vary everything in Nature. There are no two men alike—no two voices alike. . . . Because God saw fit to make some red and some white, and some black, and some brown, are we to sit here in judgment upon what God has seen fit to do?" (ibid., 16).

18.   Ibid., 57.

19.   Ibid., 176.

20.   For a reasonably accurate, though highly flattering, account of Turner's secular offices, see Mungo M. Ponton, *Life and Times of Henry M. Turner* (New York: Negro Universities Press, 1970), chapter 4.

21.   Redkey, *Respect Black*, 75.

22.   Edwin S. Redkey demonstrates indisputably that Turner wanted only the best African Americans to go back to Africa, and not the weak, non-Christian, or faint of heart. See Redkey, "Bishop Turner's African Dream," in *Black Apostles: Afro-American Clergy Confront the Twentieth Century*, ed. Randall K. Burkett and Richard Newman (Boston: G. K. Hall, 1978), 233–34. Turner wrote on one occasion: "I have said forty times that all I advocated was that five hundred million of us should go to Africa and build a civil government that would serve as an asylum for the oppressed and degraded portion of our race. I have never advocated all the colored people going to Africa, for I am well aware that the bulk of them are lacking in common sense and are too fond of worshiping white gods. I have told the country a thousand times that I favored the self-reliant Negro going and not the scullion Negro" (from Redkey, *Respect Black*, 143).

23.   For Turner's reply to Crummell, see Redkey, *Respect Black*, 161–62.

24.   Turner's removal as editor of his primary communication medium, *The Voice of Missions,* and his declining health caused him to rapidly lose his widespread influence. His removal signaled a change in the direction of radical A.M.E. policy toward what Wilmore has termed a deradicalization of black Christianity (see Wilmore, *Black Religion,* 135–40).

25.   Redkey, *Respect Black,* 163.

26.   According to Edwin Redkey, Turner went so far as to suggest that interracial unions would be the only solution to racial antagonisms that would lead, if not resolved, to "extermination, anarchy and horror." He quotes Turner as saying: "This is a gloomy picture, but there is only one thing that will prevent its realization and that is marriage between whites and blacks; social contact that will divide blood; blood that will unify and centralize the feelings, sympathy, interest, and abrogate the prejudice, race caste, color barriers and hair textures, is the only hope of our future in this country" ("Bishop Turner's African Dream," 230). However, Redkey interprets Turner as cynically musing on this point rather than actually advocating interracial unions.

27.   Ibid., 237.

28.   Redkey, *Respect Black,* 73–74.

29.   Redkey notes: "Frederick Douglass, the aging, abolitionist hero reminded *Recorder* readers that Negroes had been in America for 250 years and owed no allegiance whatever to Africa. In his view the United States provided as good a place as any for achieving equality" ("Bishop Turner's African Dream," 230).

30.   Redkey, *Respect Black,* 162.

31.   Redkey, "Bishop Turner's African Dream," 233.

32.   At least two scholars make this claim. See Wilmore, *Black Religion,* 125–29, and Redkey, "Bishop Turner's African Dream," 241.

33.   Mungo Ponton notes: "Bishop Turner had only two thoughts, namely: the freedom of his Race, and the redemption of Africa. And it made no difference upon which of these thoughts he began his discourse, he would invariably end his speech on the other. He accepted the motto of the church: God our father; man our brother, and Christ our Redeemer. That was his creed" (*Life and Times of Henry M. Turner,* 99).

34.   Angell, *Bishop Henry McNeal Turner,* 256.

35.   From "A Letter to his Son," in Redkey, *Respect Black,* 46.

36.   See Wilmore, *Black Religion,* 127. Wilmore also documents the ties that Turner created between the A.M.E. church and several independent African church movements.

37.   Henry McNeal Turner, "African Question," *Christian Recorder,* 22 Feb. 1883, as quoted in Redkey, *Respect Black,* 55.

38.   Redkey, *Respect Black,* 135.

39.   Turner's views on Washington were always ambivalent. On one hand he supported Washington's call for industrial education and his tolerance of separation from whites. On the other hand, Turner was much closer, ideologically

speaking, to W. E. B. Du Bois (Washington's main opponent) in that he called for the recognition of all human rights for blacks. For a reading of Turner in which he is interpreted as being more accepting of Washington, see Angell, *Bishop Henry McNeal Turner,* 238–42.

40.   Prominent scholars who have found Turner's work important include Cecil Wayne Cone, *The Identity Crisis in Black Theology* (Nashville: African Methodist Episcopal Church Press, 1975); Major J. Jones, *The Color of God* (Macon, Ga.: Mercer University Press, 1987), 30–31; and Gayraud Wilmore, *Black Religion.*

41.   W. E. B. Du Bois, *Crisis* (July 1915), as quoted in Wilmore, *Black Religion,* 259 n. 8.

CHAPTER 3. IDA B. WELLS–BARNETT: WOMANIST RESPONSIBILITY

1.   By the term *womanist,* I mean a responsible moral agent of the female gender who is a member of and acts on behalf of the black community. The classic definition comes from Alice Walker: "Womanist from womanish. . . . A Black feminist or feminist of color. . . . Usually referring to outrageous, audacious, courageous or willful behavior. . . . Acting grown up" (*In Search of My Mother's Garden* [New York: Harcourt, Brace and Jovanovich, 1983], xi). A black womanist theologian, Jacquelyn Grant, who has also ascribed this status to Ida B. Wells-Barnett, defines the term: "A womanist then is a strong Black woman who has sometimes been mislabeled as a domineering castrating matriarch. A womanist is one who has developed survival strategies in spite of the oppression of her race and sex in order to save her family and her people" (*White Women's Christ and Black Women's Jesus: Feminist Christology and Womanist Response* [Atlanta: Scholars Press, 1989], 205).

2.   The autobiographical information on Ida Wells-Barnett is derived from her autobiography, *Crusade for Justice,* ed. Alfreda Duster (Chicago: University of Chicago Press, 1970). A good secondary source is Emilie Townes's dissertation, "The Social and Moral Perspectives of Ida B. Wells-Barnett as Resources for a Contemporary Afro-Feminist Christian Social Ethic" (Evanston, Ill.: Northwestern University, 1989).

3.   For consistency, I will henceforth refer to Ida B. Wells by her married name, Ida B. Wells-Barnett, even when discussing her life prior to her marriage.

4.   Emilie Townes writes: "The lynching of a dear friend, Thomas Moss, launched Wells into international prominence as leader in the anti-lynching crusade. Her contribution was crucial: she spoke out at a time when few voices challenged the horror and injustice of the lynch law, and her research, writing and public speaking informed people of the facts. She was convinced that the public's awareness of the atrocity of lynching would lead to its demise" ("Ida Wells-Barnett: An Afro-American Prophet," *The Christian Century* 206, no. 9 [15 March 1989], 285).

5.   Diary of Ida B. Wells, 11 April 1887, Special Collections, Joseph Regenstein Library, University of Chicago.

6.   Wells's interpretation of the liberating action of God in the world on behalf of the marginalized is not simply revisionist history. Wells herself was

considered a prophet by the black church of that era, which clearly understood God as acting in the world and using moral agents for projects of liberation. In a sermon in 1897, Rev. Normand B. Wood wrote: "God has raised up a modern Deborah in the person of Miss Ida B. Wells, whose voice has been heard throughout England and the United States wherever it was safe for her to go. . . . We believe that same God who raised up Lincoln and Grant to 'break eery yoke, and let the oppressed go free' has raised up this courageous and eloquent young woman that in the language of the prophet, she might 'cry aloud, spare not, lift up thy voice like a trumpet, and show my people their transgressions and their sins'" *(The White Side of a Black Subject* [Chicago: American Publishing House, 1897], 381).

7.   Wells observed: "Like many another person who had read of lynching in the South, I had accepted the idea meant to be conveyed—that although lynching was irregular and contrary to law and order, unreasoning anger over the terrible crime of rape led to the lynching; that perhaps the brute deserved death anyhow and the mob was justified in taking his life" *(Crusade for Justice,* 64).

8.   Ibid., 64.

9.   The full, lurid details of this event can be found in chapter 6 of Wells-Barnett, *Crusade for Justice,* 47–52.

10.   Ibid., 51.

11.   Of the intransigence of Americans, Wells-Barnett wrote: "No matter how heinous the act of the lynchers may have been, it was discussed only for a day or so and then dismissed from the attention of the public. In one or two instances the governor has called attention to the crime, but the civil processes entirely failed to bring the murderers to justice" *(On Lynchings: Southern Horrors, a Red Record, and Mob Rule in New Orleans* [New York: Arno Press and *New York Times,* 1969], 72). As to her recognition of the power of accountability, she wrote: "Since the crusade against lynching was started, however, governors of states, newspapers, senators and representatives and bishops of churches have all been compelled to take cognizance of the prevalence of this crime and to speak in one way or another in the defense of the charge against this barbarism in the United States. This has not been because there was any latent spirit of justice voluntarily asserting itself, especially in those who do the lynching, but because the entire American people now feel, both North and South, that they are objects in the gaze of the civilized world and that for every lynching humanity asks that *America render its account to civilization and itself*" (ibid., 72; emphasis added).

12.   While crusading in England, Wells-Barnett wrote about the reactions of the British to the common American practice of segregated Christian services: "It seems incredible to them that the Christian churches of the South refuse to admit Negro communicants into their houses of worship save in the galleries or in the back seats" *(Crusade for Justice,* 155).

13.   Wells-Barnett wrote: "Eight Negroes lynched since last issue of the *Free Speech.* Three were charged with killing white men and five with raping white women. Nobody in this section believes the old thread-bare lie that negro men assault white women. If Southern white men are not careful they will over-reach

themselves and a conclusion will be reached which will be very damaging to the moral reputation of their women" (*Crusade for Justice*, 65–66).

14. Ibid., 58.

15. According to Wells-Barnett, a large proportion of streetcar riders in Memphis were black. At that time, Memphis did not have segregated streetcar service. Along with advocating emigration from Memphis, Wells-Barnett encouraged the black residents of Memphis to boycott the streetcars (ibid., 54–55).

16. Wells-Barnett wrote: "I, too, would have preferred that Mr. Douglass had chosen one of the beautiful, charming colored women of my race for his second wife. But he loved Helen Pitts and married her and it was outrageous that they should be crucified by both White and Black people for so doing" (ibid., 73.)

17. About this project Wells-Barnett wrote: "I did not think that our Christian forces should leave State Street to the devil. If we could have a modern, up-to-date reading room set down there in the midst of all those temptations, and a consecrated young man in charge of it, whose duty would be to visit the saloons and poolrooms several times a day distributing cards to the young men he found therein, inviting them to this reading room, it would be a splendid beginning in the way of having something that would help the young men who came to the city" (ibid., 303).

18. Ibid., 357.

19. The secretary of the organization was an elevator operator and the treasurer, a redcap at the Illinois Central Station. Wells-Barnett's Bible class leader was a ragpicker and junkman (ibid., 358).

20. She wrote: "It is bad enough that our leading people refuse to take part in work of this character or to know men of this type [the leaders of low social status in her organization]. But to me it is still worse that they not only refuse themselves to help, but they are doing everything that they can to disparage and to sneer at those of us who are struggling that they may keep this effort going" (ibid.).

21. The interrelationship between racial and economic oppression is crystal clear in this situation. The twelve scapegoats were black cotton farmers who had attempted to unionize and had refused to sell their cotton below the market price. Whites in the area rioted in a very sophisticated manner, such that they wound up confiscating the crops raised by black hands.

22. Wells-Barnett, *Crusade for Justice*, 402, 403.

23. In fact, the following winter she was visited by one of the twelve prisoners, who had subsequently migrated to Chicago. He related the effectiveness of her liberating gospel: "Mrs. Barnett told us to quit talking about dying, that if we really had faith in the God we worshiped we ought to pray to him to open our prison doors, like he did for Paul and Silas." After that, he said, "we never talked about dying any more, but did as she told us, and now every last one of us is out and enjoying his freedom" (ibid., 404).

24. For a description of the other-worldly aspects of black religion, see E. Franklin Frazier, *The Negro Church in America* (New York: Schocken Books, 1964).

25.   Emilie Townes, "Social and Moral Perspectives," 304.

26.   I have been much influenced on this point by the work of Emilie Townes, whose ground-breaking study on Wells-Barnett is the definitive statement to date. Townes writes: "Liberation has spiritual and social dimensions. The aim of liberation is to restore a sense of self to the oppressed as a free people and as spiritual beings. This was exhibited by Wells-Barnett time and again. Her aim was steady and relentless in its project to declare the dignity and worth of Afro-Americans" (ibid., 310).

27.   For a full discussion of Wells-Barnett as a womanist, see Townes, "Social Work and Moral Perspectives."

28.   Ibid., 329, 330.

29.   Wells-Barnett was well aware that she frequently refused to listen to other blacks. The most interesting example of this phenomenon arose when she was debunking the sexual mythology of America that systematically characterized sexual relationships between black men and white women as rape. As a result of her studies of lynching, Wells-Barnett knew that many of the charges of rape were false, and she was not too demure to say so. On or about August 3, 1894, when they had learned that she was to be interviewed by the *New York Sun,* several black men requested that she tone down her remarks with regard to the chastity of white women. She refused to do so and the published remarks created an uproar. See Wells-Barnett, *Crusade for Justice,* 220.

30.   Ibid., 311–12.

31.   Clearly, Wells-Barnett endured pain and struggled rather than passively suffering. Townes makes an illuminating distinction between suffering and enduring pain in the struggle for liberation: Townes' writes, "Wells-Barnett joins those who reject suffering as God's will and believe that it is an outrage there is suffering at all. Although the details of analyses may differ, an Afro-feminist ethic must be dedicated to eliminating suffering on the grounds that its removal is God's redeeming purpose" ("Social and Moral Perspectives," 295).

32.   Of this affair, Wells-Barnett writes: "She came and told me that her husband had gone to the general secretary of the YMCA, expecting him to deny my statement that colored young men were not admitted to that institution. He was very greatly surprised when Mr. Loring W. Messer began to excuse and explain why they were drawing the color line in the YMCA. Her husband responded by saying, "I never knew this was being done until Mrs. Barnett told my wife so, and I will never give you another dollar until you do something for colored men" (*Crusade for Justice,* 302).

CHAPTER 4. FRANCIS J. GRIMKE: RESPONSIBILIST AS PURITAN CRITIC

1.   How Grimké viewed his father is unclear. What is clear is that he recognized the systematic rape of black women in slavery to be a systemic evil: "The white race itself is not free from faults. . . . Are all white men paragons of virtue? Where did all the mulattoes in the South come from? Were the old masters forced

by their black slaves to part with their virtue, or was the reverse true? Were the slaves the aggressors, or the masters?" (*Works of Francis J. Grimké*, 1:283).

2. Grimké was proud of the pastoral legacy that he inherited: "No church in this city has been more pronouncedly outspoken in behalf of our rights. You have only to think of some of the men who have filled this pulpit—Cook, Catto, Tanner, Garnet, Martin. . . . These men were all race men and were never silent when the time came to speak out. That has been its record, and it is not likely that this record will ever be changed" ("Anniversary Address," in *Works of Francis J. Grimké,* 2:549).

3. All three responsibilists discussed in this book were proponents of what Peter Paris has called the black Christian tradition of nonracist Christian inclusivity, which is best summed up by the anachronistic phrase "The Fatherhood of God and the Brotherhood of Man." See Peter J. Paris, *The Social Teachings of the Black Churches,* (Philadelphia: Fortress Press: 1985).

4. Grimké notes: "I regard no man as a friend, I care not what his profession may be, or how many good things he may say patronizingly of the Negro, or how much money he may give for Negro education, if, by word or act, he denies the essential equality of the Negro as a man, if he looks upon him and treats him as an inferior being, belonging to a lower order of creation; if he thinks that a Negro ought to be satisfied with less than a white man is satisfied with; that there are things that white men may aspire to that Negroes have no right to aspire to. I care not, I say what he may think of himself or what others may think of him, I class him among the enemies of the race, among those who are seeking, consciously or unconsciously, to break down in the Negro that which is most essential to his true manhood—his self-respect" (*Works of Francis J. Grimké,* 1:371).

5. From an address, "The Paramount Importance of Character, or Character, the True Standard by which to Estimate Individuals and Races," delivered by Grimké on October 7, 1911. See *Works of Francis J. Grimké,* 1:488. Grimké's theology did not blind him to the racial advantages that whites held in his era, "That the possession of a white skin in the United States gives a man a decided advantage over a man with a dark skin, is true, in that the white man has privileges, opportunities, advantages open to him that are not open to the man of darker hue; but that does not affect in the least the fact that with God a white skin carries no more weight than a black skin, or a skin of any other hue. With him, race, color, makes neither for nor against an individual or race" (ibid., 1:480).

6. Ibid., 1:487–88. At the same time Grimké insisted that the "colored" people of his day be proud of their color: "Never be ashamed of the fact that you are identified with the colored race. And never let the colored race be ashamed of the fact that you are a part of it. Be upright, straightforward, honorable in all your dealings. Only by so living can you be a credit to yourself or to your race" (ibid., 3:157).

7. Grimké writes: "What our enemies are seeking to effect is to make this a white man's government; to fix permanently our status in it, as one of civil and political inferiority. This issue is sharply drawn; and it is for us to say whether we

will be thus reduced, whether such shall be our permanent status or not" (ibid., 1:400).

8.   In criticizing Washington for eschewing racial integration and for siding with white segregationists, Grimké wrote: "Mr. Washington has been too ready to sacrifice the rights of his race for a temporary material advantage. Out of such a spirit there never can come the highest moral and spiritual development. Men who stress, as he does, success as measured by mere material well-being, are never exponents of a lofty morality, theoretically or practically. They move on the lower plane of the material, and estimate things by material values or standards" (ibid., 3:8).

9.   Grimké was a realist; he recognized the low status of blacks of his era and urged others to do the same. He urged blacks to help themselves, "so that whether the Negro wants to remain a separate and distinct people in this country or not, the simple fact is he cannot help himself. He is separate, has been, and is likely to be for many years to come" (ibid., 2:552).

10.   Grimké's pessimism with regard to the possibility of whites helping blacks coupled with the call for blacks to lift themselves up on their own foreshadowed the self-help positions of certain modern black conservatives. Compare with Walter Williams, *All It Takes Is Guts* (New York: Regenery Books, 1987).

11.   See *Works of Francis J. Grimké,* 2:553.

12.   Ibid.

13.   Grimké notes: "If the Negro is ever to make any headway in this direction, there must be cooperation, he must be sustained through the patronage of his own people, and his own people must sustain him, not simply because they may be interested in him as an individual, but because it is a race enterprise, involving larger interests than the immediate profits that may accrue to the individual running the business. The success of the enterprise means much to the individual owner, but it means vastly more to the race" (ibid.).

14.   Perhaps Grimké's elitism is best exemplified in his agreement with Bishop Daniel Payne and Booker T. Washington on the subject of the poor preparation of many black southern ministers. One of the foremost ministers of his era and the founder of Wilberforce University, Payne was torn by his own criticism of many of his A.M.E. ministers and was not supported in this matter by Bishop Henry McNeal Turner, but rather by Grimké. In a reminiscence of Payne, Grimké wrote: "The same spirit showed itself again in his endorsement of what Prof. B.T. Washington said about the intellectual and moral unfitness of a very large class of colored ministers." Elsewhere Grimké also wrote of some black ministers: "Many of them are ignorant men; men who can scarcely do more than read and write. Some of them can hardly do that. Many of them are ungodly men; men who are in the pulpit purely from selfish considerations; for what they can get out of it; and they are ready at all times to fall in with anything that will advance their personal and selfish interests, regardless of how it may affect the welfare of the people. . . . The statement made by Professor Washington, sometime ago, as to the intellectual and moral unfitness of a large proportion of our ministers, created a great sensation . . . but the simple fact is, his statement has never been refuted." Grimké's

support of Payne was grounded in his commitment to excellence, although his inclination to elitism prevented him from sharing the more pragmatic, realistic assessment of Bishop Turner, who more accurately assessed the enormous need during their era for even modestly educated ministers. The controversy in the A.M.E. church on this matter was mediated and settled by Bishop Turner, who consolidated a reconciliation. For Grimké's full remarks, see *Works of Francis J. Grimké*, 1:26, 28. For a reference to Turner's position see, Angell, *Bishop Henry McNeal Turner*, 196–97.

15. "There is a duty here, devolving upon our educated classes with reference to those who are not so far advanced as themselves, which, I am afraid, has been but little appreciated. As we rise in the scale, the light that emanates from us, the kind of life we live ought to be a guide and an inspiration to those who are coming on behind" (*Works of Francis J. Grimké*, 2:555).

16. Ibid., 2:556, 557.

17. Yet, for his frequent lectures at black colleges, Grimké often refused to accept an honorarium, which was merely designed to cover his travel expenses (*Works of Francis J. Grimké*, 1:xvii).

18. See *Works of Francis Grimké*, 2:556. Elsewhere, however, Grimké writes: "The wise race leader is the man or woman who sees what these higher things are, and who is laboring to turn the thoughts of the race more and more towards them. It will be helpful to us, therefore, if we will pause and allow the great teacher to instruct us on this point. What has He to say about life, individual life, racial life? He says, It does not consist in things; it does not consist in the abundance of things that may be possessed. That is the great truth which Jesus here holds up, and which it is important for us, as a race, to remember and lay to heart. And it is important just now particularly, because, unfortunately, the very opposite of that is the gospel which is being preached. What the Negro needs, we are told, is to amass wealth, to buy property, to get hold of the soil, to have a bank account, and everything will be all right. That is not what the Lord Jesus says, though that is what some of our race leaders are asserting" (1:379).

19. Grimké recognized that modern capitalists fervently pursued the acquisition of capital as a calling that was no longer connected to any religious source but rather constituted an irrational obsession. He did not, however, appreciate the irrationality of capitalism and the ethical dilemmas it could create, particularly for people who wanted to be virtuous, generous Christians. For a description of the transition from traditional mercantilism to capitalism, see Max Weber, *The Protestant Ethic and the Spirit of Capitalism* (New York: Charles Scribner & Sons, 1958).

20. Grimké's sermons are peppered with illustrations of people from the bottom of society who make good. Reading from newspaper clippings, he would tell his congregation about the success of hard-working people: "The spirit exhibited by this young man and these young women, the disposition to qualify themselves, to do well the work committed to them, is just the spirit that we need and must have if we are to succeed" (*Works of Francis J. Grimké*, 2:562).

21.   For a description of communitarianism, see Jeffrey Stout's insightful work, *Ethics after Babel: The Languages of Morals and Their Discontents* (Boston: Beacon Press, 1988), 224–36.

22.   The Invisible Hand refers to the guidance of the individual by the free market, in which the selfishness of the individual intent on building a better mousetrap works to the benefit of society, despite the fact that the individual had no intention of conferring this benefit.

23.   *Works of Francis J. Grimké*, 3:45. I am indebted to Louis B. Weeks III for calling this aspect of Grimké's thought to my attention. For Weeks's insightful article, see "Racism, World War I and the Christian Life: Francis J. Grimké in the Nation's Capital," in *Black Apostles: Afro-American Clergy Confront the Twentieth Century*, ed. Randall K. Burkett and Richard Newman (Boston: G. K. Hall, 1978), 57–75.

24.   Eventually, Grimké refused to attend meetings of presbytery when they were held in the countryside where his color made him a pariah. At the same time, he staunchly opposed the reunion of the southern and northern Presbyterian churches, since the terms for such a reunion were tantamount to imposing second-class citizenship on the black ministers in the new unified denomination. For an insightful review of Grimké's views on reunion, see Henry Justin Ferry, "Racism and Reunion: A Black Protest by Francis James Grimké," *Journal of Presbyterian History* 50, no. 2 (Summer 1972), 77–88. Similarly, Grimké had to refuse to engage in the practice of pulpit exchanges, since all such exchanges invariably resulted in his being assigned other colored pulpits exclusively. He interpreted these actions as refusals to recognize his full standing as a minister of the Gospel solely on the basis of his skin color. See *Works of Francis J. Grimké*, 4:91–116.

25.   Grimké often preached to integrated audiences, so that the whites of his generation had opportunities to hear from a representative of the oppressed. In one such sermon, he wrote: "I have had a three-fold object in preaching these sermons: (1). To let the white people know that we are conscious of what our rights are, and that we mean to have them. (2). The hope of helping to awaken the sleeping conscience of the American people to the wrongs that we are suffering. And (3) to inspire those of our own people, who may be disposed to become despondent, with hope and with renewed determination to keep up the struggle" (*Works of Francis J. Grimké*, 1:290).

26.   Ibid., 1:517.

27.   Grimké simply did not fully understand that white Christians of his era did not really believe that God is no respecter of persons—that is, that their Christianity was racist. As a consequence, he ascribed his understanding of Christianity (which was nonracist) to Wilson, who had no such convictions. His subsequent criticism of Wilson for not holding to his convictions was wrongheaded, since it focused on Wilson's alleged hypocrisy rather than on the true cause of Wilson's racist leadership—his uncritical embrace of inherently racist American religion and culture. When Grimké wrote in his second and critical letter to Wilson that "all class distinctions among citizens are un-American, and the sooner every

vestige of it is stamped out the better it will be for the Republic," he was simply expressing views that Wilson never had (ibid., 1:518).

28.   In one of his sermons, Grimké ruefully notes: "In the block where I am living, which is one of the longest blocks in the city, a few years ago every house in it, on both sides, was occupied by white people; today there is only one white family to be found in it. There has been an almost complete exodus. Just as soon as one colored family got in, the excitement began; and when a second got in it created almost a panic. One by one these white people, 'Folded their tents like the Arabs, And silently stole away'" (ibid., 1:460). Grimké accepted the intransigent racist nature of the white flight and did not follow the white exodus into other parts of the Washington, D.C., area. Instead, he remained within his marginalized community.

29.   Ibid., 2:552.

30.   Ibid., 1:446.

31.   Ibid., 3:75.

32.   Ibid., 3:79.

33.   Grimké offers an extensive interpretation of the "Fatherhood of God and the Brotherhood of Man" (ibid., 1:447–48).

34.   Ibid., 1:470.

35.   Ibid., 1:275.

36.   Ibid., 1:276.

37.   For Grimké's opposition to lynching, see chap. 3, "The Lynching of Negroes in the South: Its Causes and Remedies," in ibid., 1:291–317.

38.   Grimké believed that the struggle for liberation was to be grounded in prayer to the God of liberation. At the same time, he believed in intercessory prayer for oppressors: "Prayer can help us in this struggle,—let us lay hold of it. Let us make the most of it. But . . . in praying we must not stop with self, we must not forget to pray also for those who are oppressing us, who have their heels upon our necks, and whose cry is 'this is a white man's government.' Jesus himself says, 'Pray for them which despitefully use and persecute you'" (ibid., 1:286).

39.   Blyden was publicly supported by Bishop Henry McNeal Turner. Neither Blyden nor Turner were able to get Grimké to endorse widespread African emigration.

40.   Although this fault was not highlighted in the examination of Henry McNeal Turner (see chap. 2), it must be said that he too was a slave to Horatio Alger enthusiasms.

41.   Grimké was much more interested in bringing the Gospel to the poor than he was in analyzing the causes of poverty. Christian approaches that appeared to lift the poor out of their degradation met with his approval. See his laudatory remarks on Hugh Sherwood's *God in the Slums* in *Works of Francis J. Grimké*, 3:500.

42.   Grimké relied on Du Bois for much "secular" theory, but he believed that any critical analysis that was not grounded in Christianity was inherently suspect. Of Du Bois he writes: "Men, like Du Bois, when they speak on economics, or on the civil and political rights of the Negro as an American citizen, speak with

authority and may be safely followed; but when it comes to religion and morality, they are sadly in need of guidance themselves. They are far, far out of the way as tested by the Word of God and the ideals and principles of Jesus Christ. Their views are distorted, perverted, erroneous. To follow them is to be misled, to be facing in the wrong direction. Not being right themselves, they are incapable of pointing out the way to others" (ibid., 3:465).

43.   Marable, *Capitalism,* 147.

44.   He was so beloved and venerated that he was never really able to resign his pulpit.

45.   If the so-called truly disadvantaged are considered (as it is hoped this book does), the viability of at least some African Americans remains tenuous.

CHAPTER **5.** RESPONSIBLE SELVES IN MARGINALIZED COMMUNITIES: THE VARIETY OF RESPONSES

1.   See chap. 1.

2.   A review of Niebuhr's work reveals little consideration of the need to meet basic human needs or the need to recognize human rights. For this reason, the linking of responsibilist ethics to the movement to meet basic human needs is a process that must be conducted by a new generation of responsibilists.

3.   Some of the problems in regard to this needs analysis have to do with the tendency of a free-market society systematically and unrestrainedly to create needs for market commodities. Andrew Bard Schmookler writes of this phenomenon: "The ideology of the market economy has obscured the psychological problem of our addiction to wealth by teaching us that human beings are insatiable by nature and that limitless appetite, being natural, is good. 'Economic Man' is presumed to have infinite wants, and economic theory would have us believe that the millionth dollar of a person's consumption is as valuable as the first. Wealth and human fulfillment have become equated in the predominant ideology of liberal society, even though the great spiritual teachers of humanity have taught otherwise" ("The Insatiable Society: Materialistic Values and Human Needs," *The Futurist* [July–Aug. 1991], 17–18).

4.   Nancy Fraser, "Talking about Needs: Interpretive Contests as Political Conflicts in Welfare-State Societies," *Ethics* 99, no. 2 (Jan. 1989): 291.

5.   Ibid., 292.

6.   David Braybrooke, *Meeting Needs: Studies in Moral, Political, and Legal Philosophy* (Princeton: Princeton University Press, 1987), 36.

7.   Ibid., 36. Braybrooke's list is indeed odd in that it does not specifically mention two of the most widely recognized needs: the need for freedom and the need for the free exercise of religion. It is also unusual in that is does not mention cultural needs.

8.   Ibid, 60.

9.   Again, the best illustration of this is Braybrooke's own list, which, though extensive, does not even list freedom or religion as basic human needs.

10.   Alan Gewirth, *Human Rights: Essays on Justification and Application* (Chicago: University of Chicago Press, 1982), 20.

11.   The ancient nomadic custom of extending hospitality to any visitor for at least three days, which is frequently noted in the Old Testament, is not a rights-oriented practice; instead, it is a duty-oriented practice that is unrelated to rights claiming.

12.   Fraser, "Talking about Needs," 296.

13.   See Paul Althaus's standard work on Luther, *The Ethics of Martin Luther* (Philadelphia: Fortress Press, 1972), 106.

14.   Martin Luther, *Luther: Selected Political Writings,* ed. J. M. Porter (Philadelphia: Fortress Press, 1974), 77.

15.   Ibid., 72.

16.   The unpersuasive nature of Luther's position is easy for the modern citizen of a democracy to understand. Government authority resides with the people in present-day United States, a country that was created out of a war of revolution against what was perceived to be colonial oppression—bad government. The notion of a justified revolution was inconceivable to Luther, who was living in a country made up of unstable principalities perched on the edge of the industrial revolution. Althaus describes Luther's position on bad government: "Those who govern sit in God's place. Therefore disobedience and rebellion against the government are disobedience and rebellion against God himself. When governments punish, God's own wrath is at work. This is the case even though officials are often 'knaves and rascals' who misuse their office, act arbitrarily, and perpetrate injustice" (*Ethics of Martin Luther,* 113–14).

17.   Luther, *Political Writings*, 80.

18.   For a typical example of this approach, see Samuel Baah's essay entitled, "The Genesis of Human Needs," in *The Church in Response to Human Need,* ed. Vinay Samuel and Christopher Sugden (Grand Rapids, Mich.: Eerdmans, 1987), 226–33.

19.   Niebuhr, *Christ and Culture,* 211.

20.   Ibid., 212.

21.   In reference to Pope Pius XI, Hollenbach writes: "All of Pius XI's claims about respect for persons' claims to material, bodily and even psychological necessities are ultimately founded on a characteristic of the person which transcends any and all of these needs. Persons have needs which must be respected. But these needs must be respected because human beings in their radically personal constitution are more than a collection of needs. They are spiritual or transcendental as well as material beings, and must never be totally subordinated to the functional desires or needs of other persons" (*Claims in Conflict: Retrieving and Renewing the Catholic Human Rights Tradition* [New York: Paulist Press, 1979], 51–52).

22.   Niebuhr subscribed to the notion that human selves have infinite worth, but only by virtue of the concomitant assertion that their infinite worth was due to their being regarded as valuable beings by an infinite being, the One beyond the Many (see *Meaning of Revelation,* 110).

23. Like Hollenbach, Holleman constructs a basic human needs approach from his interpretation of Catholic social teachings. Citing a variety of papal encyclicals and analyzing the work of Catholic human rights scholars, including that of David Hollenbach, Holleman criticizes several philosophical arguments that are opposed to meeting basic needs: "What is lacking, in these essays and in most others in the volume, is the argument that food and shelter are important as ends in themselves, that God has endowed the physical dimension with as much dignity as the pneumatic, that being in good health would be important even if it were not a prerequisite to the fulfillment of life plans or the exercise of free speech" (*The Human Rights Movement: Western Values and Theological Perspectives* [New York: Praeger, 1987], 120).

24. Drew Christiansen, "Basic Needs: Criterion for Development" in *Human Rights in the Americas: The Struggle for Consensus*, ed. Alfred Hennelly and John Langan (Washington, D.C.: Georgetown University Press, 1982), 257.

25. Pope John Paul II, *On the Hundredth Anniversary of Rerum Novarum: Centesimus Annus* (Washington, D.C.: United States Catholic Conference, 1 May 1991), 67.

26. Niebuhr, *Responsible Self,* 98–99.

27. Ibid., 99.

28. Ibid., 100.

29. For such a reading of Nietzsche, see Henry Shue's comments on the subject in *Basic Rights: Subsistence, Affluence, and U.S. Foreign Policy* (Princeton: Princeton University Press, 1980), 18.

30. See Matt. 6:9–13.

31. See Matt. 2:13–21.

32. Matt. 9:10–13 and 11:18–9.

33. Matt. 12:9–14.

34. Ibid.

35. Matt. 12:1–8.

36. Luke 7:36–40.

37. For an examination of Gnostic expressions of Docetism, see Arthur Cushman McGiffert, "A Short and Easy Way with Heretics," in *A History of Christian Thought, Vol. 1: Early and Eastern: From Jesus to John of Damascus* (New York: Charles Scribner's Sons, 1960), 149–55.

38. Modern famines are often unnatural. Instead of being caused by a cyclical downturn in rain or the onslaught of pests or even the destruction wrought by horrible weather, many are caused by a disruption in a region's agriculture due to war, economic conditions or other factors.

39. Niebuhr, *Responsible Self,* 65.

40. With regard to the difference between internal and external history, Niebuhr writes: "The distinctions between the two types of history cannot be made by applying the value-judgment of true and false but must be made by reference to differences of perspective" (*Meaning of Revelation,* 46).

41. Matt. 25:31–46.

42.   Niebuhr, *Radical Monotheism*, 108–9.

43.   What kinds of relationships we enter into has an impact on the level of our moral responsibility. A useful work by Joseph L. Allen is probably the best text for understanding the varieties of covenants that are formed and the range of social and moral responsibilities that are possible between the great variety of groups that make up the world. See *Love and Conflict: A Covenantal Model of Christian Ethics* (Nashville: Abingdon Press, 1984).

44.   With regard to external history, Niebuhr writes: "It appears, first of all, that the data of external history are all impersonal; they are ideas, interests, movements among things. Even when such history deals with human individuals it seek to reduce them to impersonal parts. Jesus becomes, from this point of view, a complex of ideas about ethics and eschatology, of psychological and biological elements. Other persons are dealt with in the same manner" (*Meaning of Revelation*, 47).

45.   Niebuhr, *Responsible Self*, 80.

46.   Ibid., 83.

47.   The very meaning of America is subject to widely varying interpretations that accentuate differences between an internal historical perspective and an external one. The clearest and one of the most celebrated examples is that of Frederick Douglass with reference to the meaning of the Fourth of July: "What to the American slave is your Fourth of July? I answer, a day that reveals to him more than all other days of the year, the gross injustice and cruelty to which he is the constant victim. To him your celebration is a sham; your boasted liberty an unholy license; your national greatness, swelling vanity; your sounds of rejoicing are empty and heartless; your denunciation of tyrants, brass-fronted impudence; your shouts of liberty and equality, hollow mockery; your prayers and hymns, your sermons and thanksgivings, mere bombast, fraud, deception, impiety, and hypocrisy—a thin veil to cover up crimes which would disgrace a nation of savages" (*My Bondage and My Freedom* [Chicago: Johnson Publishing Co., 1970], 349–53).

CHAPTER **6.** FACING THE INHERENT LIMITATIONS OF RESPONSIBILITY

1.   John Bennett, a noted Christian ethicist, with whom the use of middle axioms is often associated, describes them as "more concrete than a universal principle and less specific than a program that includes legislation and political strategy" (*Christian Ethics and Social Policy* [New York: Charles Scribner & Sons, 1946], 77).

2.   The main reason for the difficulty lies in the inherently selfish nature of social groups and moral communities. Most ethicists insist that although individuals may have some natural inclinations to act in altruistic ways, groups do not. For a classical statement on this issue, see Reinhold Niebuhr, *Moral Man and Immoral Society* (New York: Charles Scribner, 1932). For a recent statement on this problem, see Peter Paris's inaugural address, "Expanding and Enhancing the Moral Communities: The Task of Christian Social Ethics," *Princeton Seminary Bulletin* 7, no. 2 (June 1986), 148–49.

3. Niebuhr, *Responsible Self,* 162–63.

4. Robert Michael Franklin, *Liberating Visions: Human Fulfillment and Social Justice in African-American Thought* (Minneapolis: Augsburg Fortress, 1990), 13.

5. Raboteau, *Slave Religion,* 140.

6. Of this period, Gayraud Wilmore writes: "In British possessions, such as Barbados and Jamaica, where the former Georgia slave, Reverend George Liele, founded the first Baptist church in Kingston in 1782, black congregations helped to create a climate for rebellion in the early nineteenth century by developing new forms of leadership based upon church government among the slaves. The leaders of the insurrections in Demerara in 1823 and Jamaica in 1831 were strongly supported by church members" (*Black Religion,* 106).

7. Liele's example should not be understood to be superior to that of other moral exemplars. His act of temporary self-alienation is paradigmatic only in the sense that all responsible selves are called to make sacrifices. Thus his acceptance of slavery and indentured servitude do not constitute legitimation of such practices or an encouragement that other would-be responsibilists imitate his acts. By implication, Liele's action does call into question the stance taken by James Cone that moral responsibility requires immediate and visible resistance to all forms of oppression.

8. One writer who maintains that modern international exchanges, as presently constituted, impoverish weak traders is Susan George. See *A Fate Worse Than Debt* (London: Pelican Books, 1988).

9. Merely to outline these concerns would be an enormous task; in fact, setting out the inherent international implications of a full-fledged responsibilist approach would in itself justify a book-length study.

10. Wilson, *The Truly Disadvantaged,* 7.

11. This black abandonment of the inner city has not escaped the notice of other scholars. C. Eric Lincoln and Lawrence H. Mamiya note that "some studies have pointed out the increasing bifurcation of the black community into two main class divisions: a coping sector of middle-income working-class and middle-class black communities, and a crisis sector of poor black communities, involving the working poor and the dependent poor. The demographic movement of middle-income blacks out of inner city areas and into residential parts of the cities, older suburbs, or into newly created black suburbs, has meant a growing physical and social isolation of the black poor. For example, since the 1960s, 48 percent of the black population of Atlanta has moved out of the central city into surrounding counties. The gradual emergence of two fairly distinct black Americas along class lines—of two nations within a nation—has raised a serious challenge to the Black Church. . . . In past generations some of the large urban black churches were one of the few institutions that could reach beyond class boundaries and provide a semblance of unity in black communities. The challenge for the future is whether black clergy and their churches will attempt to transcend class boundaries and reach out to the poor, as these class lines continue to solidify with demographic changes in black communities" (*The Black Church in the African American Experience* [Durham, N.C.: Duke University Press, 1990], 384). If black out-migration to the suburbs

continues at its current pace, this problem will worsen with every succeeding generation.

12.   Even if the actions of a Lang were replicated on a national scale, they might not be sufficient to begin to address some of the chronic, long-term problems inherent in a modern managerial capitalist state. Nevertheless, such actions are indeed appropriate or fitting responses. For a description of Lang and his work, see Diane Dismuke, "Realizing the American Dream," *NEA Today* 7, no. 10 (October 1988), 10.

13.   Freire, *Pedagogy of the Oppressed,* 3.

EPILOGUE: DELICATE ALLIANCES—CONFLICTING MOTIVATIONS
AND "FITTING ACTS"

1.   This particular problem has been fully explored by Paris, *Social Teachings of the Black Churches,* 57–82.

2.   This work suggests two outstanding projects. One consists of a more systematic statement of a theology that focuses on the meeting of basic human needs. The other, more foundational, project is a sociologically oriented study or conversation with a representative group of our most marginalized citizens. The former project would seem to be predicated upon the viability of the latter. The latter project would require an editor writing on behalf of others who are probably better at living morally responsible lives in covenanted Christian communities that are oppressed than they are at writing about such experiences. The work might be entitled *Voices of the Formerly Silenced: Confessions of Transcending Responsibilists.*

Selected Bibliography

Allen, Joseph L. *Love and Conflict: A Commercial Model of Christian Ethics*. Nashville: Abingdon Press, 1984.

Althaus, Paul. *The Ethics of Martin Luther*. Philadelphia: Fortress Press, 1972.

Angell, Steven Ward. *Bishop Henry McNeal Turner and African-American Religion in the South*. Knoxville: University of Tennessee Press, 1992.

Baah, Samuel. "The Genesis of Human Needs." In *The Church in Response to Human Needs,* edited by Vinay Samuel and Christopher Sugden, 226–33. Grand Rapids, Mich.: Eerdmans, 1987.

Bennett, John C. *Christian Ethics and Social Policy*. New York: Charles Scribner's & Sons, 1946.

Braybrooke, David. *Meeting Needs: Studies in Moral, Political, and Legal Philosophy*. Princeton: Princeton University Press, 1987.

Cannon, Katie G. *Black Womanist Ethics*. Atlanta: Scholars Press, 1988.

Christiansen, Drew. "Basic Needs: Criterion for Development." In *Human Rights in the Americas: The Struggle for Consensus,* edited by Alfred Hennelly and John Langan. Washington, D.C.: Georgetown University Press, 1982.

Cone, Cecil Wayne. *The Identity Crisis in Black Theology*. Nashville: African Methodist Episcopal Church Press, 1975.

Cone, James H. *A Black Theology of Liberation*. New York: Orbis Press, 1990.

———. *God of the Oppressed*. New York: Seabury Press, 1975.

De Santa Ana, Julio. *Towards a Church of the Poor: The Work of an Ecumenical Group on the Church and the Poor*. New York: Orbis Press, 1981.

Doenecke, Justus D. "H. Richard Niebuhr: Critic of Political Theology." *Communio* 4 (Spring 1977): 83–93.

Douglass, Frederick. *My Bondage and My Freedom*. Chicago: Johnson Publishing Co., 1970.

Du Bois, W. E. B. *The Souls of Black Folk*. New York: Signet Classics, New American Library, 1969.

———. *W. E. B. Du Bois Speaks, 1890–1919,* edited by Philip Foner. Vol. 1. New York: Pathfinder Press, 1970.

Ferry, Henry Justin. "Racism and Reunion: A Black Protest by Francis James Grimké." *Journal of Presbyterian History* 50, no. 2 (Summer 1972): 77–88.

Fowler, James. *To See the Kingdom: The Theological Vision of H. Richard Niebuhr*. Nashville: Abingdon Press, 1974.

Fraser, Nancy. "Talking about Needs: Interpretive Contests as Political Conflicts in Welfare-State Societies." *Ethics* 99, no. 2 (Jan. 1989): 291–313.

Frazier, E. Franklin. *The Negro Church in America*. New York: Schocken Books, 1964.

Freire, Paulo. *Pedagogy of the Oppressed*. Translated by Myra Ramos. New York: Seabury Press, 1970.

Gardner, E. Clinton. *Biblical Faith and Social Ethics*. New York: Harper & Brothers, 1960.

———. "Responsibility and Moral Direction in the Ethics of H. Richard Niebuhr." *Encounter* 40, no. 2 (Spring 1979): 143–68.

George, Susan. *A Fate Worse Than Debt*. London: Pelican Books, 1988.

Gewirth, Alan. *Human Rights: Essays on Justification and Application*. Chicago: University of Chicago Press, 1982.

Grant, Jacquelyn. *White Women's Christ and Black Women's Jesus: Feminist Christology and Womanist Response*. Atlanta: Scholars Press, 1989.

Grimké, Francis J. *The Works of Francis J. Grimké: Addresses Mainly Personal and Racial,* edited by Carter G. Woodson. Washington, D.C.: Associated Publishers, 1942.

Gutiérrez, Gustavo. *The Power of the Poor in History*. Translated by Robert R. Barr. Maryknoll, N.Y.: Orbis Press, 1984.

Habermas, Jürgen. *Communication and the Evolution of Society*. Boston: Beacon Press, 1979.

Hollenbach, David. *Claims in Conflict: Retrieving and Renewing the Catholic Human Rights Tradition*. New York: Paulist Press, 1979.

———. *The Church in Response to Human Need*. Grand Rapids, Mich.: Eerdmans, 1987.

Jones, Major J. *The Color of God*. Macon, Ga.: Mercer University Press, 1987.

Kelly, John. "Time for the Grace of Doing Nothing." *The Christian Century* 105, no. 31 (26 Oct. 1988), 940–41.

Kelsey, George D. *Racism and the Christian Understanding of Man*. New York: Charles Scribner's Sons, 1965.

Lincoln, C. Eric, and Lawrence H. Mamiya. *The Black Church in the African-American Experience*. Durham, N.C.: Duke University Press, 1990.

Marable, Manning. *How Capitalism Underdeveloped Black America: Problems in Race, Political Economy and Society.* Boston: South End Press, 1983.

Míguez Bonino, José. *Toward a Christian Political Ethics.* Philadelphia: Fortress Press, 1983.

Moseley, Romney. *Becoming a Self before God: Critical Transformations.* Nashville: Abingdon Press, 1991.

Niebuhr, H. Richard. *Christ and Culture.* New York: Harper & Row, 1975.

———. "The Grace to Do Nothing." *The Christian Century* 49 (23 March 1932), 378–80.

———. *The Meaning of Revelation.* New York: Macmillan, 1960.

———. *Radical Monotheism and Western Culture.* New York: Harper & Row, 1970.

———. *The Responsible Self.* New York: Harper & Row, 1963.

———. *Social Sources of Denominationalism.* New York: New American Library, 1957.

Niebuhr, Reinhold. *Moral Man and Immoral Society.* New York: Charles Scribner's, 1932.

Oglesby, Enoch. *Ethics and Theology from the Other Side: Sounds of Moral Struggle.* Lanham, Md.: University Press of America, 1979.

Paris, Peter J. "Expanding and Enhancing the Moral Communities: The Task of Christian Social Ethics." *Princeton Seminary Bulletin* 7, no. 2 (June 1986), 145–56.

———. *The Social Teachings of the Black Churches.* Philadelphia: Fortress Press, 1985.

Ponton, Mungo M. *Life and Times of Henry M. Turner.* New York: Negro Universities Press, 1970.

Pope John Paul II. *On the Hundredth Anniversary of Rerum Novarum: Centesimus Annus.* Washington, D.C.: United States Catholic Conference (1 May 1991).

Raboteau, Albert. *Slave Religion.* New York: Oxford University Press, 1978.

Redkey, Edwin S. "Bishop Turner's African Dream." In *Black Apostles: Afro-American Clergy Confront the Twentieth Century,* edited by Randall K. Burkett and Richard Newman, 227–46. Boston: G. K. Hall, 1978.

Redkey, Edwin S., ed. *Respect Black: The Writings and Speeches of Henry McNeal Turner.* New York: Arno Press, 1971.

Schmookler, Andrew Bard. "The Insatiable Society: Materialistic Values and Human Needs." *The Futurist* (July–Aug. 1991), 17–21.

Stewart, Carlyle F., III. *God, Being and Liberation: A Comparative Analysis of the Theologies and Ethics of James H. Cone and Howard Thurman.* Lanham, Md.: University Press of America, 1989.

Townes, Emilie. "Ida Wells-Barnett: An Afro-American Prophet." *The Christian Century* 106, no. 9 (15 March 1989), 285–86.

———. "The Social and Moral Perspectives of Ida B. Wells-Barnett as Resources for a Contemporary Afro-Feminist Christian Social Ethic." Ph.D. Diss., Northwestern University, Evanston, Ill., 1989.

Turner, Henry McNeal. "African Question." *Christian Recorder* (22 Feb. 1883).

Walker, Alice. *In Search of My Mother's Garden.* New York: Harcourt, Brace and Jovanovich, 1983.

Weber, Max. *The Protestant Ethic and the Spirit of Capitalism.* New York: Charles Scribner & Sons, 1958.

Weeks, Louis B. "Racism, World War I and the Christian Life: Francis J. Grimké in the Nation's Capital." In *Black Apostles: Afro-American Clergy Confront the Twentieth Century,* edited by Randall K. Burkett and Richard Newman. Boston: G. K. Hall, 1978.

Wells-Barnett, Ida B. *Crusade for Justice,* edited by Alfreda Duster. Chicago: University of Chicago Press, 1982.

———. "The Crusade Justified." In *On Lynchings: Southern Horrors, a Red Record, and Mob Rule in New Orleans.* New York: Arno Press and *New York Times,* 1969.

West, Cornel. *Prophesy Deliverance! An Afro-American Revolutionary Christianity.* Philadelphia: Westminster Press, 1982.

Wilmore, Gayraud. *Black Religion and Black Radicalism: An Interpretation of the Religious History of Afro-American People.* Maryknoll, N.Y.: Orbis Books, 1989.

Wilson, William J. *The Truly Disadvantaged: The Inner City, the Underclass, and Public Policy.* Chicago: University of Chicago Press, 1987.

Wood, Normand B. *The White Side of a Black Subject.* Chicago: American Publishing House, 1897.

Index

Abandonment, black, 98
Accommodationism: and Grimké, 52; and Turner, 25; and Booker T. Washington, 42
Accountability: Grimké's understanding of, 54; Niebuhr's understanding of, 4; Turner's problems with, 28, 29, 30; Wells-Barnett's understanding of, 40, 41; with regard to the white community, 55

Braybrooke, David, 68, 69

Capitalism, 60, 61
Christiansen, Drew, 78
Christology: Grimké's, 56, 57, 58; Niebuhr's, 6, 7; Turner's, 31, 32; Wells-Barnett's, 43, 44
Cone, James: and Christology, 13; and criticisms of Niebuhr, 13; and non–intervention, 17; and suffering, 12; and the will of God, 12, 13
Conscientization, 100

"Disadvantaged, the truly," 1
Discourse, political, 73
Double consciousness, 9
Du Bois, W. E. B. *See* Double consciousness; Self

Ethics of survival, 81
External history, examples of, 87

Fraser, Nancy: and basic human needs, 66, 67. *See also* Discourse, political
Freire, Paulo. *See* Conscientization

Gardner, E. Clinton. *See* Will of God
Gewirth, Alan. *See* Principle of Generic Consistency
Grimké, Francis J., 49–62; and rights; 18, and divine duties, 18; and his understanding of the self, 50; and divine initiative, 52; and opposition to repatriation of African Americans, 52, 53; and capitalism, 60, 61
Guilt, 90

7762-6
5-23